MW01070104

The Islamic Classical Library
MADRASA COLLECTION

Handbook on Islam

By

Shaykh 'Uthman dan Fodio
Translated by Aisha 'Abdarrahman Bewley

DIWAN PRESS

Classical and Contemporary Books on Islam and Sufism

Copyright © Diwan Press Ltd., 2017 CE/1439 AH

Handbook on Islam

Published by:	Diwan Press Ltd.
	311 Allerton Road
	Bradford
	BD15 7HA
	UK
Website:	www.diwanpress.com
E-mail:	info@diwanpress.com

Author:	Shaykh 'Uthman dan Fodio
Translation:	Aisha Bewley
Cover design by:	Abdassamad Clarke

A catalogue record of this book is available from the British Library.

ISBN-13:	978-1-908892-52-2 (Casebound)
	978-1-908892-51-5 (Paperback)

Printed and bound by:	Lightning Source

Table of Contents

Biography of
Shaykh 'Uthman dan Fodio

Shaykh 'Uthman dan Fodio

'Uthman ibn Muhammad ibn 'Uthman ibn Salih, the author of the *Kitab Usul ad-Deen* and the *Kitab 'Ulum al-Mu'amala,* was born in Maratta in Gobir on the last day of Safar, 1168 AH (15 December 1754). He became known as Uthman dan Fodio (son of Fodio). Fodio, in the Fulani language, means "learned" and was a name given by the people to his father Muhammad who was a scholar and the first teacher of the Shaykh, instructing him in the Qur'an.

During his childhood his father settled in a place called Degel, some fifty miles north of modern Sokoto, and it is here that Shaykh Uthman lived for most of most of his life. After studying with his father, Uthman dan Fodio went on to other teachers including his relative, the scholar 'Uthman Binduri, staying with him about two years and moulding himself to his pattern of piety, enjoining the right and forbidding the wrong. From him, he went to Jibril ibn 'Umar in Agades.

Shaykh Jibril was a Berber of North African origin who had come to settle among the Tuareg of the Southern Sahara. Uthman dan Fodio gave himself up entirely to his Shaykh and gained through him great knowledge, enabling him in his turn to pass on this pure teaching. Shaykh Jibril was known for his absolutely uncompromising Islam and also for the fierceness with which he communicated it to the Tuareg tribesmen about him. Uthman dan Fodio, while equally uncomprising, is remembered for the gentle-

1

ness with which he treated his followers. After he had been with Shaykh Jibril for only a year, the Tuareg became so discomfited by the presence of Shaykh Jibril in their midst that they forced him to leave and he went on *Hajj* to Makka. Uthman dan Fodio returned from Agades to Degel.

Uthman dan Fodio began teaching others when he was only twenty years old and still studying. By passing on what he had learned he followed the traditional practice of Muslim scholarship, both studying and teaching simultaneously. Throughout his life, he taught openly, accepting all who came. He taught people according to their capacity and in a language that all could understand. His following, which grew rapidly, consisted mainly of ordinary people and the nobility. Few scholars visited him or showed enthusiasm for his community. Their desire was for a more exclusive brand of scholarship, consisting of the reading of obscure classical texts in a narrow circle, while the Shaykh's work was to communicate the basic teachings of Islam to as many people as possible.

His most famous book, *Ihya' as-Sunna* (The Giving Life to the Practice) instructs people in the daily practices of Islam as shown in the life of the Prophet Muhammad, may Allah bless him and grant him peace. His life was the fulfillment of his book. He spoke against pagan practices that had been introduced by so-called Muslim rulers and against other abuses of power, calling people of the clear straight way laid down in the Qur'an and illustrated by the practice of the Prophet and the life of his companions in the first Muslim community.

He spent most of his time at Degel and established there a functioning Muslim community consisting of his family and followers. The community was quite large, comprising at least sixty-two households, including his brother 'Abdullah and several scribes, scholars and Qur'an reciters. Shaykh Uthman's life was very simple. He avoided property, living without wealth or servants. He would occasionally go into retreat, though only for short periods. During this time he received *karamat* which he describes in his book, *Lama Balaghtu*.

Many would come from far away to stay with him, learning and absorbing. Afterwards, with instructions from the Shaykh, they would return to their homes to spread to others the knowledge of Islam they had acquired. In this way the influence of Shaykh Uthman was felt far and wide. He himself confined his movements mainly to the area surrounding Degel, holding gatherings and teaching the people. Every night of *Jumu'a* he held meetings for invocations and teaching at Degel. He avoided the courts of the rulers and advised his followers to do the same.

His increasing popularity alarmed the rulers themselves, and in 1202 AH (1788) Shaykh Uthman was summoned by the Sultan of Gobir to go to Magami for the prayer of *'Id al-Kabir*. After the prayer all the Sultan's scholars, numbering about a thousand in all, left him to join the Shaykh. Although it is said that his original intention had been to kill the Shaykh, the Sultan agreed to five conditions proposed by the Shaykh:

1) That he should be allowed to call people to Allah without hindrance.
2) That none should be stopped from following him.

3) That any man wearing a turban should be treated with respect.
4) That all prisoners should be freed.
5) That the subjects of the Sultan should not be overburdened with taxes.

This agreement put the Shaykh and the Muslim community in a very strong position and enabled him to teach and send his students to teach far and wide, establishing Islam wherever they went.

Ten years later, however, after this Sultan, Bawa, had died, a new Sultan, Nafata, clamped down on the Muslim community. He issued a proclamation:

1) Only the Shaykh was to be permitted to teach.
2) No son could be converted away from his father's religion.
3) All who had become Muslims were to return to the religion of their fathers.
4) No one was to be permitted to wear a turban or a veil.

This was a direct attack against the Muslim community and it marks the beginning of the *Jihad* (armed struggle).

The Shaykh did not respond directly to this hostility, and continued to teach. When Nafata's son, Yunfa, became Sultan of Gobir, he tried to have him killed, influenced by his courtiers who felt that their power and authority were being threatened by the expansion of the Muslim community. The attempt on his life was not successful, and it was at this time that the Shaykh wrote a book called *al-Masa'il Muhimma* (Important Questions). In it it clearly stated the obligation of *hijra* (emigration and *jihad* for the Muslims when they are threatened by pagans.

Under the threat of attack by the Gobirawa army, the Muslims made *hijra* Northwest to a place called Gudu. It was February, a time of year when food and water were scarce, and the Muslims, despite having been armed in self-defence for six years, were not fully prepared either for travel or war. Yunfa became alarmed at the numbers joining the Shaykh and he forbade further emigration, harassing those who tried to go and confiscating their property. Confrontation was now inevitable, and the Muslims prepared their defences and elected a leader. Despite reluctance on the part of the Shaykh, and his insistance that he was not strong enough to bear the burden of a *Jihad*, the Shaykh was formally chosen as Khalif of the community and *Amir al-Mu'minin*.

The first skirmish occurred when a small punitive expedition from Gobir was beaten back. After this the Muslims captured two towns, Mantakari and Konni, and the Shaykh had to appoint his close companion, 'Umar al-Kammu as Treasurer to the community to make sure that the spoils were distributed according to the *Shari'a* (the injunctions of Islam). Finally, the Muslims met the full Gobirawa army led by the Sultan at a place called Kwotto. The Muslims were outnumbered and not equipped to face the heavy cavalry of the enemy, but they were fighting for Allah and the establishment of Islam, and after a fierce fight the Gobirawa were routed.

After this victory, support for the Muslims increased considerably and they were able to travel more freely in the land. For the most part they were successful in the fighting. Eventually, after travelling some seven hundred miles over a period of eighteen months, the Muslims built a permanent base for the Shaykh.

In the meantime Shaykh Uthman's son, Muhammad Bello, had been sent by his father to meet with Muslim leaders from Katsina, Kano, Daura and Zamfara. He read a letter from the Shaykh greeting the leaders and inviting them to make *ba'ya* (an oath of allegiance) with the Khalif as the Qur'an and *Sunna* demanded. The letter also contained counsel. The leaders accepted the Shaykh's authority. In this way most of what is now northern Nigeria became included in the Shaykh's community.

The campaigning continued and Islam spread to the South and the East. Finally, in 1223 AH (1808) Alkalawa, the capital of Gobir, the great stronghold of the enemies of the Muslim community, fell, and the Sultan was killed. Most of the inhabitants accepted Islam, and those who did not fled to the North. With the fall of Alkalawa, resistance to the Muslims was broken everywhere, and the Khalifate of Shaykh Uthman dan Fodio was firmly established in the land.

Shaykh Uthman had previously written a small book about administration and what was necessary for it in a Muslim community. This is what was set up in the various Amirates throughout the Khalifate. Apart from the Amir who acted as governor and was responsible for collecting the *zakat* (poor tax), the other officials that he considered necessary were a *Qadi* (judge), an Imam and one man called a *Muhtasib* was responsible for overseeing all the others, making sure that none exceeded or skimped in their appointed tasks. The Shaykh appointed Amirs in every part of the Khalifate. They were known as flagbearers since they each carried a flag that had been blessed by the Shaykh. Each would carry a letter of instruction from the Shaykh.

Shaykh Uthman was able to return to his work of teaching and writing, which he did day and night. All his books are of immediate relevance and guidance to the people of his community. His oral teaching was against oppression and misuse of power. He warned against extortion from the poor and condoning the crimes committed by one's own household. As always, he continued to convey to people the basic teachings of Islam.

From Gwandu he moved North to Sifawa, where he stayed for five years. In 1230 AH (1815) he moved to Sokoto where his son established a town. He died there on 3 *Jumada al-Akhira* (20 April 1817) at the age of 63. As he had meticulously followed his beloved Prophet, may Allah bless him and grant him peace, during his life, so he followed him in death, dying at the same age.

Since the beginning of man's history a clear pattern can be seen. Time after time one man arises in his community, calling his people to the Truth, to the worship of One God. He shows them how to worship and how to live. He gives them the good news of the reward of the Garden in the Next Life for those who accept and follow him, and warns them of the terrible punishment of the Fire in the Next Life for those who reject him and turn away. These men were the Prophets and Messengers sent by the Creator of the Universe as a mercy and guidance for man, the most noble of His creatures.

The final Messenger who brought for all people the last and most perfect Way was Muhammad, upon him be peace and blessings. Since his death, men have appeared in different places at different times renewing his way and calling men back to it. They are the men who have given themselves up entirely to their Lord, and they have in turn been chosen to transmit the teaching to those around them, and around them has sprung up a rebirth of Islam.

Shaykh Uthman dan Fodio is one of these men. His whole life bears this out. His only concern was the spreading of the teaching of Islam and calling people to the Truth, to Allah, demonstrating by his words and his actions the teaching and the practice of the Prophet Muhammad, may Allah bless him and grant him peace. He was a man utterly unconcerned with power or wealth, and his entire time was spent teaching, writing, and counselling others to Truth, may Allah cover him with mercy and give him the best of rewards. To this day his light persists, and in those places where his flags were planted, the tree of Islam continues to flourish.

Abdalhaqq Bewley

The Kitab 'Usul ad-Deen
The Foundations of the Life-Transaction

by
Shaykh 'Uthman dan Fodio,
may Allah cover him with mercy. Amen.

In the name of Allah, the Merciful, the Compassionate

May Allah bless our Master Muhammad
and his family and Companions and
grant them perfect peace.

Says the slave, the poor man in need of the mercy
of his Lord, 'Uthman ibn Muhammad ibn 'Uthman,
known as Dan Fodio, may Allah cover him with
mercy, Amin:

Praise belongs to Allah, Lord of all the worlds,
and blessings and peace be upon the Messenger of
Allah, may Allah bless him and grant him peace.

This book is called the *Foundations of the Life-transaction* and will be of use, if Allah wills, to all who
look to it for support. I say - and success is by Allah -
that the whole universe, from the Throne to the
spread carpet of the earth, is situated in-time and its
Maker is Allah, may He be exalted! His existence,
may He be exalted! is necessary - from before end-
less-time without beginning, going on forever, without end. He is not comparable to any being in-time.
He has no body and no attributes of body. He has no
direction and no place. He is as He was in pre-exis-
tence before the universe came into being. He is
wealthy beyond dependence on place or designation.
He is One in His Essence and in His Attributes and
in His Actions. He is powerful by means of His
power, He wills by means of His will, He knows by
means of His knowledge, He is living by means of
His life, He hears by means of His hearing, He sees
by means of His sight, and He speaks by means of
His speech. He has complete freedom as to whether
He acts or leaves undone. All Divine perfections are

His by necessity. Any deficiency, the opposite of divine perfection, is entirely impossible for Him.

All the Messengers from Adam to Muhammad, may Allah bless all of them and grant them peace, are truthful and trustworthy and they conveyed what they were commanded to convey to creation. All human perfection is theirs by necessity and all human imperfections are impossible for them. Permitted to them are eating, drinking, marriage, buying and selling, and any illness which does not lead to imperfection.

The angels are all preserved from wrong-action. They do not disobey Allah in anything He commands and they carry out all that they are commanded to do. They are made of light and are neither male nor female. They neither eat nor drink.

The Books from Heaven are all true and truthful. Death at its appointed time is true. The questioning of the inhabitants of the graves by Munkar and Nakir and others is true. The punishment of the grave is true. The ease of the grave is true. The Day of Rising is true. The awakening of the dead on that day is true. The gathering of the people in one place on that day is true. The giving of the books is true. The weighing of actions is true. The Reckoning is true. The narrow bridge is true. Drinking from *Kawthar* is true. The Fire is true. The endlessness of the Fire with its people is true. The Garden is true. The endlessness of the Garden with its people is true. The vision of Allah by the believers in the Next World is true. Everything that Muhammad, may Allah bless him and grant him peace, came with is true.

These are the foundations of the Life-transaction. Allah has confirmed them all, divinity, prophethood

11

and the Next World, in the Vast Qur'an. All who are responsible must believe in them just as they have come to us. In the case of the common people simple belief in and acceptance of all these tenets is sufficient. In the case of the elite, they form the basis of further knowledge. This is because of the difficulty the common people have in understanding proofs.

As it was said by 'Izz'ud-Din, Sultan of the scholars, in *The Foundations of the Sciences and the Islam of the People*, "For that reason the Messenger of Allah, may Allah bless him and grant him peace, did not make those who became Muslims delve into these things. Instead he would make them firm since it was known that they would be separated from him. This was the way followed by the Rightly-guided Khalifs, and rightly-guided scholars still establish these foundations in this way."

As for those who are among the people of inner sight, they must reflect on these foundations in order to abandon blind following and become convinced with the eye of the heart. This is in order that the life-transaction of the people of inner sight should be based on clear vision, particularly for those who reach the station of calling others to Allah. Allah says, "*Say: This is my way. I call to Allah with inner sight, I and whoever follows me.*"

Here ends the *Book of the Foundations of the Life-transaction*.

O Allah! Give us success in following the *sunna* of Your Prophet Muhammad, may Allah bless him and grant him peace. O Allah! Bless our master Muhammad, and the family of our master Muhammad, and grant him abundant peace.

The Kitab 'Ulum al-Mu'amala
The Book of the Sciences of Behaviour

by
Shaykh 'Uthman dan Fodio,
may Allah cover him with mercy. Amin.

In the name of Allah, the Merciful, the Compassionate

May Allah bless Sayyiduna Muhammad
and his family and Companions, and
grant them peace abundantly.

So says the poor man in need of his Lord's mercy,
'Uthman b. Muhammad b. 'Uthman, known as Dan
Fodio, may Allah cover him with His mercy!

Praise belongs to Allah, the Lord of the worlds,
and blessings and peace be upon the Seal of the
Prophets, and on all his family and Companions. I
bear witness that there is no god but Allah, alone,
without partner, and I bear witness that Muhammad
is His slave and Messenger, the best of the first and
the last, with a witnessing upon which we will die
and upon which we will be raised up, Allah willing,
among the trustworthy ones.

This is *The Book of the Sciences of Behaviour.*

It is in three parts:

1) **ISLAM** - the science of *fiqh*, concerning the outward aspects of the *deen*.
2) **IMAN** - the science of *tawhid*, concerning the
beliefs comprising the foundations of the *deen*.
3) **IHSAN** - the science of *tasawwuf*, concerning
the inward aspects of the *deen*.

1
ISLAM
the Science of *Fiqh*

Every responsible person must learn as much of it as is necessary for him to be able to fulfil his obligations.

Unit 1: Purification

Allah says, *"We sent down pure water out of the sky."*

Pure water is needed for all acts of purification. This means water which is both pure in itself, and able to purify other things - such as rain-water, sea-water and well-water. It must not have been changed in any of its three basic qualities (colour, taste and smell) by anything which might have been added to it, like milk, honey, oil, ghee, grease, fat, soap, filth, urine, or excrement. If any of the three qualities we have mentioned has been changed, it is not acceptable to use it for *istinja'* (cleaning yourself from urine or faeces), *wudu'* (ablution) or *ghusl* (major ablution).

Water which has been changed by the addition of something pure can be used for ordinary purposes but not for acts of *'ibada* (worship). If it is changed by something impure, it cannot be used either for ordinary purposes or for acts of *'ibada*. If it is changed by something occurring naturally at its bed, like earth or salt, or by something that grows in it like water-moss, or by the length of time it has stood, it is not impaired and it can be used for ordinary things and for acts of *'ibada*.

15

If something impure falls into a small amount of water - a vessel for doing *wudu'* or a jug for *ghusl* - and it does not change it, it is acceptable to purify yourself with it. However, doing so is disliked if other water can be found. Water which has already been used for *wudu'* or *ghusl* is considered pure, but using it is disliked if other water can be found. There are two conflicting statements about water which has been used for things other than *wudu'* or *ghusl* - like that used for cooling or for washing the hands.

Section 1

Every living thing is pure, human or otherwise, together with its sweat, saliva, nasal mucous, tears, and eggs (unless they are rotten - then they are changed and putrid). Human milk is pure. It is permitted to consume the milk of animals whose meat is normally eaten, such as cattle, sheep, and camels, and it is pure. The urine and dung of such animals are also pure as long as they have not been exposed to any impurity. Other types of milk go according to the meat of the animal concerned. If the meat of an animal is *haram* to eat, its milk is impure.

All dead bodies including human corpses - except in the case of the Prophets - are impure with the exception of certain insects. Human urine and faeces are also impure - except in the case of the Prophets - as is the urine and excrement of every animal which it is *haram* to eat and those animals which it is disliked to eat - such as beasts of prey and wolves. Suppuration and pus, blood flowing from humans or any other creature, and vomit which has been changed from its state of food are also impure. Intoxicants (like wine), sperm, genital discharge, prostatic fluid, and the ashes of a burned impurity are also impure.

Section 2

Any impurity must be removed from the clothes of those intending to pray, and also from their bodies and from the place of prayer (those places with which their bodies are going to make contact), if they are aware of it and are able to remove it with free flowing water. If only a minute amount of water is used and then the prayer is done, the prayer is invalid. The same applies if you remember that there is an impurity on your garment, your body, or prayer-place during the course of the prayer; you must break off the prayer, remove the impurity and begin again. If there is an impurity at the place where you are praying but a thick pure covering is placed over the top of it, it is absolutely permitted to pray there - whether you are sick or healthy. This is according to Ibn Yunus in his classification of what is preferred.

Section 3

A little blood, whether it is your own or from something else and whether it is from menstruation, lochia, or some other cause, which you see during the prayer is generally overlooked. The same applies to a small amount of pus or suppuration. A small amount is what is less than the size of a small coin. You can also overlook the flow from the popping of a boil if it has not been squeezed, and the blood of fleas, and mud from wet ground, even if there might be manure in it, unless it is known to be from a source which is mostly manure.

Unit 2: The Obligations of *Wudu'*, its *Sunan* (Traditions), and What Breaks it

The Obligations of *Wudu'*

The obligations of *wudu'* are seven in number:

1) **Intention**. The first is intention which takes place in the heart. When you begin to wash your face, you make a clear intention to perform the obligatory duty of *wudu'*, or to remove a ritual impurity (*hadath*) to make permissible what the impurity prevented you from doing.

2) **Face**. The second is to wash all of the face which is from the normal hair line at the top of the forehead to the point of the chin lengthwise and, in width, everything between the two ears. When washing the face, make sure the water gets into any wrinkles on the forehead or elsewhere and that it covers the surface of your lips and the ridge between the nostrils. You must make the water penetrate the hair of your beard if it is light but if it is thick, you can wipe over it.

3) **Hands and arms**. The third is to wash the hands and arms up to the elbows. You must make the water go between your fingers.

4) **Head**. The fourth is to wipe over the whole head. The head begins at the top of the forehead where the face ends and ends at the base of the skull.

5) **Feet**. The fifth is to wash the feet including the ankles. It is recommended to make water go between the toes.

6) **Rubbing.** The sixth is to rub, which means that every part covered in *wudu'* must be rubbed with the hand as well as covered with water.

7) **Continuity.** The seventh is to continue without interruption. This means to do *wudu'* all at one go without any excessive break, with presence and thoroughness.

The *Sunnas* of *Wudu'*

The *sunnas* of *wudu'* are eight in number.

1) **Hands.** The first is to wash the hands.

2) **Mouth.** The second is to rinse the mouth. This is to take water into the mouth, and move it around, and then spit it out.

3) **Sniffing up.** The third is to sniff up. That is to draw water right up into the nose.

4) **Blowing out.** The fourth is to blow out. That is to blow the water out while holding the nose with the index finger and thumb of the left hand.

5) **Ears.** The fifth is to wipe the ears, externally and internally.

6) **Fresh water for it.** The sixth is to take fresh water for wiping the ears.

7) **Returning the hands.** The seventh is to bring the hands back to the front when wiping the head.

8) **Correct order.** The eighth is to follow the correct order of the obligations of *wudu'*, starting with the face, then the forearms, then wiping the head, then washing the feet.

Note

If you leave out one of the obligations of *wudu'* you must repeat *wudu'* and then repeat the prayer. If you leave out one of the *sunnas*, you should repeat *wudu'*, but you do not have to repeat the prayer.

Description of *Wudu'*

When you do *wudu'*, you begin by saying, *"Bismillah"* (In the name of Allah), and place the water on your right side where you can reach it. You begin by washing your hands before putting them into the water container. Then you take water with your right hand and rinse your mouth out three times - with one handful if you like, or with three handfuls. If you rub your teeth with your right index finger, it is good. Then you sniff up water into your nose and blow it out three times. You hold your nose with your left hand as you blow out. If you do these actions less than three times it does not matter and you can do it all with one handful of water, but it is better and safer to do each action three times with fresh water each time.

Then you take water with both hands - or, if you like, with your right hand, pouring it onto both your hands - and wash your face thoroughly with them, from the top of your forehead - whose limit is the beginning of the hair-line - to the tip of your chin, and around all of your face from the end of the longest part of your beard to your temples. You should run your hand over the recesses of your eyelids, the lines of your forehead, and underneath the nose between the nostrils. You do this three times. You do not have to make water penetrate the beard during *wudu'*, unless it is it is so thin that you can see the skin through it, but you run your wet hand over its length.

Then you wash your right hand and forearm three times. You let water flow on it and rub it with your left hand. You make the water go between the fingers by running the fingers of your left hand between them. Then you wash your left hand and arm in the same way. You wash up to and including your elbows. It is also said that you can wash up to the elbows as the limit of the washing. It is not obligatory to include them, but including them is more thorough in making sure that you fulfil the limits.

Then, taking water with your right hand and pouring it onto your left, you wipe over your head. Placing your fingertips together on your head and putting your thumbs on your temples, you begin at the front, from the start of the hair line, and draw your hands over your head to the nape of your neck. Then you bring them back again to the front. You can put your thumbs behind your ears and bring them back to the temples. The important thing is to cover your entire head. If you put your hands into the vessel and then lift them out while they are wet and wipe your head with them, that is enough. Women also wipe in the way which we have mentioned and they must wipe over their tresses and not over their head covering. They should put their hands under any tresses which extend beyond the napes of their necks when they bring their hands back to the front.

Then, pouring water onto your thumbs and index fingers - or, if you like, dipping them into the water - you wipe the outside and inside of your ears with them.

Then you wash your feet. With your right hand you pour water onto your right foot and rub it thoroughly with the left hand. You do that three times. If you like, you can make water go between your toes but if you do not, there is no objection. However, making water go between them is better and preferred by the *'ulama'*. You should rub your heels and Achilles tendons and places where the water does not readily penetrate such as callouses and cracks. A good way to do it is to rub while pouring out the water with the other hand. The saying has reached us, "Woe to the heels because of the Fire!" The heel of a thing is its extremity and end. Then you do the same with your left foot.

Fixing the washing of the limbs at three times is not by a command and less than that is permissible as long as you perform *wudu'* thoroughly. People are not all the same in that respect.

The Messenger of Allah, may Allah bless him and grant him peace, said "Whoever does *wudu'* and does it well, and then raises his finger to the sky and says, 'I testify that there is no god but Allah, alone, with no partner, and I testify that Muhammad is His slave and Messenger,' the gates of the Garden are opened for him and he can enter by whichever gate he chooses."

Section: What Breaks *Wudu'*

There are two categories of things which break *wudu'*: ritual impurities (*hadath*) and other causes (*asbab*).

The ritual impurities are: urine, faeces, wind, prostatic fluid and genital discharge.

The causes are: sleep, loss of consciousness for whatever reason, doubt about your *wudu'*, leaving Islam, touching the penis with the inside of the hand, and touching a woman.

Sleep can be of four kinds:

1) A long heavy sleep. This breaks *wudu'*.
2) A short heavy sleep. This breaks *wudu'*.
3) A short light sleep. This does not break *wudu'*.
4) A long light sleep. After this, it is recommended to do *wudu'*.

A light sleep is reckoned to be one from which you come to with a start if your name is spoken.

Doubt can be of two kinds:

1) Doubt about doing *wudu'*.
2) Doubt about breaking *wudu'*.

If you remember breaking *wudu'* and have any doubt at all that you have done it since, you must do *wudu'*.
However, if you remember doing *wudu'* and do not remember if you have broken it or not, you only need to redo your *wudu'* if your doubt is more than fifty-fifty.

Touching a woman is also divided into four divisions:

1) If you intend sexual pleasure and experience it, you must do *wudu'*.
2) If you experience sexual pleasure without wanting to, you must do *wudu'*.
3) If you intend sexual pleasure and do not experience it, you must do *wudu'*.
4) If you do not intend sexual pleasure and do not experience it, you do not have to do *wudu'*.

Wudu' is also generally broken by kissing, even if you would not say that there was any sexual pleasure in it.

Wudu' is not broken by touching the buttocks or the testicles, and it is also not broken by touching the penis through a covering, even if it is only a light covering. In our *madhhab*, it is not broken by a woman touching her private parts although it is said that if she inserts her hand between her labia, she must do *wudu'*.

Unit 3: The Obligations of *Ghusl* (Major Washing), its *Sunan*, and its Description

The Obligations of *Ghusl*

There are five obligations of *ghusl* :

1) **Intention.** This is that you intend to remove the impurity of *janaba* (major ritual impurity).
2) **Entire Body.** In *ghusl* the entire body must be covered with water.
3) **Rubbing.** Every part of the body must be rubbed as well as made wet.
4) **Continuity.** The whole act of *ghusl* must be completed without interruption.
5) **Hair.** In *ghusl* the water must penetrate right to the roots of your hair and beard.

The *Sunnas* of *Ghusl*

There are four *sunnas* of *ghusl* :

1) **Hands.** The first is to wash the hands to the wrist.
2) **Mouth.** The second is to rinse the mouth.

3) **Nose.** The third is to sniff water up the nose.

4) **Ears.** The fourth is to wipe the ears.

Description of *Ghusl*

You should begin *ghusl* by washing your private parts and washing off any impurity you have on your body. Then you do *wudu'* in the normal way except that, if you want, you can wash your feet at this point or, if you want, you can delay washing them until the end of your *ghusl*.

Then you dip your hands into the water, lift them out without holding any water in them, and work them into your scalp. Then you wash your head thoroughly making sure that the water gets right to the roots of your hair. Women do the same and move their hair about but they do not have to unravel their braids if they have them.

Then you pour water over your right side, and then over your left side, rubbing with your hands after pouring the water until you have rubbed all of your body. If you have doubts about the water having covered any part of your body, go over it again with water. You should rub the inside of the navel and under your throat, and make water penetrate the hair of your beard. You should be careful to cover the area under your arms, your buttocks, the crooks of your elbows, behind your knees, and the soles of your feet. Water must go between your fingers.

Then at the end, if you did not do so in the beginning, you must wash your feet to complete your *wudu'*. You must take care not to touch your penis with the inside of your hands while you are rubbing. If you do so, you must do *wudu'* again, after finishing your *ghusl*.

Unit 4: The Obligations of *Tayammum* (Dry-Purification), its *Sunan* and its Description

The Obligations of *Tayammum*

There are eight obligations of *tayammum* :

1) **Intention.** In the case of *tayammum* it is particularly important to intend to make the prayer permissible because, as is well-known, *tayammum* does not remove ritual impurity.
2) **Face.** The second is to wipe the whole face.
3) **Pure Earth.** The third is using pure earth.
4) **Continuity.** The fourth is to continue without interruption.
5) **Striking the Earth Once.** The fifth is the first striking of the earth with the hands.
6) **Hands to the Wrists.** The sixth is to wipe the hands up to the wrists.
7) **Conjunction with the Prayer.** The seventh is doing it immediately before the prayer.
8) **After the Time.** The eighth is doing it after the time for the prayer.

The *Sunnas* of *Tayammum*

There are three *sunnas* of *tayammum* :

1) **Order.** The first is the proper order.
2) **Striking the Earth Twice.** The second is to strike the earth a second time for the hands.
3) **Arms to the Elbow.** The third is to wipe above the wrists up to elbow.

Description of *Tayammum*

You first strike the earth with your hands. If any earth remains on them, you can shake them lightly. Then you wipe all over your face with them in one single wiping making sure you cover all of it.

Then you strike the earth again with your hands and wipe your right hand with the left. You put the palm of your left hand on the tips of the fingers of your right hand and then slide it down the outside of your right forearm to the elbow, curving your fingers around it. Then you put your left palm on the inside of your right arm at the elbow and slide it back up until you reach the wrist. Then you slide the inside of your left thumb over the back of your right thumb and then in turn between all the fingers of your right hand. You do the same thing with your left hand and arm and then after finishing it, you draw the left palm across the right to the end of the fingers.

If anyone in a state of *janaba*, or a woman who has reached the end of menstruation, cannot find any water for purification, then they should do *tayammum* and pray. However, a man cannot have intercourse with his wife who has been separated from him by the blood of menstruation or lochia with the purification of *tayammum*. He must wait until water is found, and the woman has purified herself with it.

Tayammum can be done instead of *wudu'* on a journey, when no water can be found, and, in case of illness, when using water would make the illness worse or delay recovery.

Pure earth is considered to be anything which naturally forms the surface of the earth such as soil, sand, rock, gravel, salt flats etc. Grass, or anything which grows on the earth's surface, may not be used.

Unit 5: Menstruation and Lochia

Menstruation

Menstruation is the issuing of blood by itself from the vagina of a woman and it normally occurs roughly every four weeks for a period of up to fifteen days although it is usually less and could be even for as little as a few hours. The minimum period of the duration of menstruation is without limit and the maximum period of purity between periods of menstruation is also without limit. The minimum period of purity is fifteen days and the maximum length of menstruation varies with different women.

If it is a woman's first period, the maximum period of menstruation is fifteen days. If a woman has regular periods, she should add up to three days on to the time that her period would normally stop if unsure and then she is considered pure, provided it does not exceed fifteen days. If her period varies, she goes by the maximum length of her normal period and adds three days to that. She is considered to be menstruating during the days when she is looking to see whether her period has ended or not. If it extends up to fifteen days, she is considered pure.

If a woman is pregnant, the maximum period length for her after three months is when the bleeding reaches fifteen days. After six months, it is ten days. If the bleeding stops earlier than the time that her period would normally have finished, the earlier days are considered to have been false menstruation and she must make up any prayers she has missed.

Purity from Menstruation

Purity has two signs. The first is dryness - that is

when a woman inserts a rag into her private parts and it comes out dry, with no blood or white discharge on it. This discharge is a fine white liquid which comes at the end of menstruation and looks like lime. The discharge is a more conclusive sign for any woman who has regular periods. When she sees dryness, she should wait for the discharge at the end of the normal time. In the case of a woman who is having her first period, she should not wait for the discharge if she sees dryness first. Women should look to see if they have become pure before going to sleep and at the time of the dawn prayer.

Menstruation prevents prayer, fasting, divorce, touching the Qur'an, entering a mosque, and any sexual activity involving the private parts during the time of menstruation and after it until the woman concerned has purified herself with water. It also prevents *tawaf*. However a menstruating woman is permitted to recite Qur'an from memory.

Lochia

Lochia is blood which issues from the vagina after childbirth. It cannot last more than sixty days. If the bleeding does continue beyond sixty days, a woman should consider herself pure, the bleeding no longer being considered part of lochia. *Ghusl* at the end of lochia is the same as when a woman ends her menstrual period. There is absolutely no difference. If the blood stops before sixty days - even if it is on the very day of childbirth, the woman concerned should do a *ghusl* and pray. If the bleeding resumes but there is fifteen days between the two periods of bleeding, the second is considered to be the onset of menstruation. Periods of bleeding which are closer together than that are considered part of the lochia.

Unit 6: The Times of Prayer and its Conditions

The Times of Prayer

The time of *Dhuhr* (the noon-prayer) is from immediately after the time the sun reaches its zenith until the time when an object's shadow is equal to its length, assuming the sun to be more or less overhead at the time of noon. The time of *'Asr* (the afternoon-prayer) is from the time when the shadow is twice the length of an object to the yellowing of the sun. The time in which the prayer must be done (or it will be missed) is up until sunset. The time of *Maghrib* (the sunset-prayer) is the amount of time in which it can be prayed after the conditions of *Maghrib* are fulfilled (i.e. the complete setting of the sun). The time of *'Isha'* (the night-prayer) is from the time when the twilight disappears up until the end of the first third of the night. The time in which the prayer must be done is before the coming of dawn. The time of *Subh* (the morning-prayer) is from the first light of dawn up until the glow of the sun is visible in the eastern sky. The time in which the prayer must be done is up until the rising of the sun. You have to make up anything outside that.

Preferred (*ikhtiyari*) Time and Obligatory (*daruri*) Time of the Prayer

It will have been seen from what has preceded that the time for the prayers is divided into two parts: the beginning of the time, when it is best to do the prayer, and a later time when it is essential that the prayer be prayed to avoid missing the time altogether. Whoever delays a prayer until the latter time without any excuse has acted wrongly. A valid excuse is something like menstruation, lochia, disbelief, youth, insanity, fainting, sleep, or forgetfulness.

The Conditions of the Prayer

The conditions of prayer are six:

1) **Purification.** The first condition is purification from ritual impurity and purifying the garment, body, and place from all impure substances.
2) **Purity throughout the Prayer.** The second is purity from ritual impurity at the beginning of the prayer and throughout it.
3) **Covering the Body.** The third is covering the private parts with something substantial. A man's private parts are from his navel to his knee. A free woman's private parts are her entire body except for her face and palms.
4) **Facing the *Qibla*.** The fourth is facing *qibla*, except in battle when there is close combat, and also excepting the superogatory prayers on a journey during which the obligatory prayers are permitted to be shortened - and while the person is mounted.
5) **Not Talking.** The fifth is not saying anything that is not part of the prayer.
6) **Avoidance of Extra Movements.** The sixth is to avoid frequent unnecessary movements.

Unit 7: The Obligations of the Prayer, its *Sunan*, its Description, and What Invalidates it

The Obligations of the Prayer

There are fifteen obligations in the prayer:

1) **Intention.** The first obligation is intention. You must intend with your heart to enter into the specific prayer concerned.
2) *Takbir al-Ihram.* The second is the *Takbir al-Ihram.* It is to say clearly the words, "*Allahu Akbar*" without lengthening the *ba'*. With this you enter the prayer.
3) **Standing for it.** The third is to stand upright when you say it.
4) **The *Fatiha*.** The fourth is the recitation of the *Fatiha* either by the Imam or by anyone praying on his own.
5) **Standing during it.** The fifth is to stand upright while reciting the *Fatiha*.
6) *Ruku'.* The sixth is *ruku'* (bowing).
7) **Rising from it.** The seventh is to stand upright again from the bowing position.
8) *Sujud.* The eighth is *sujud* (prostration) twice in each *rak'at*.
9) **Sitting Back.** The ninth is to sit back between the prostrations.
10) **Following the Imam.** The tenth is the intention to follow the Imam in the prayer.
11) **Correct Order.** The eleventh is to follow the correct order, which is to start with the *Takbir al-Ihram* and the standing, to do *ruku'* before

sujud, and *sujud* before the final *salam* (greeting).

12) **Stillness.** The twelfth is that there must be at least a moment of stillness in all the fundamental positions of the prayer - standing, *ruku'*, rising from it, each *sujud*, and between the two prostrations.

13) **Correct Proportion.** The thirteenth is the correct proportion between the fundamental positions of the prayer so that as well as there being stillness in each position, each position is also clearly distinct and properly performed.

14) **The *Salam*.** The fourteenth is the *salam* (greeting) which constitutes the end of the prayer.

15) **Final sitting.** The fifteenth is the final sitting which accompanies the *salam*.

The *Sunnas* of the Prayer

There are eighteen *sunnas* in the prayer.

1) **The *Sura*.** The first is the *sura* after the *Fatiha* when appropriate.

2) **Standing for it.** The second is to stand upright while reciting it.

3) **Reciting Outloud.** The third is audible recitation during the prayers of *Subh*, *Maghrib* and *'Isha* and any other prayer which demands it.

4) **Reciting Silently.** The fourth is to recite silently during all prayers other than these.

5) **The *Takbirs*.** The fifth is every *takbir* besides the *Takbir al-Ihram*.

6) *Sami'a'llahu...* The sixth is the saying of, "*Sami'a'llahu liman hamidah,*" (Allah hears whoever praises Him) and "*Rabbana wa lakalhamd,*" (Our Lord and to You is the praise) by the Imam and those following him and someone praying on his own.

7) **First *Tashahhud*.** The seventh is the first *tashahhud* (witnessing) during the sitting at the end of the second *rak'at*.

8) **Second *Tashahhud*.** The eighth is the second *tashahhud* during the last sitting of the prayer if it is longer than two *rak'ats*.

9) **Text of the *Tashahhud*.** The ninth is the words which make up the *tashahhud* which are: "*At-tahiyyatu lillahi'z-zakiyatu lillahi't-tayyibatu's-salawatu lillah. As-salamu 'alayka ayyuha'n-nabiyyu wa rahmatu'llahi wa barakatuh. As-salamu 'alayna wa 'ala 'ibadillahi's-salihin. Ash-hadu an la ilaha illa'llahu wahdahu la sharika lah, wa ash-hadu anna Muhammadan 'abduhu wa rasuluh.*"

(Greetings belong to Allah, pure things belong to Allah, good prayers belong to Allah. Peace be upon you, O Prophet, and the mercy of Allah and His blessings. Peace be upon us, and upon the right-acting slaves of Allah. I testify that there is no god except Allah, alone with no partner, and I testify that Muhammad is His slave and Messenger)

10) **The Prayer on the Prophet.** The tenth is the prayer on the Prophet, may Allah bless him and grant him peace, which is said at the end of the final *tashahhud*. It is: "*Allahumma salli 'ala Muhammadin wa 'ala ali Muhammadin kama sallayta 'ala Ibrahima wa 'ala ali Ibrahim*

wa barik 'ala Muhammadin wa 'ala ali Muhammadin kama barakta 'ala Ibrahima wa 'ala ali Ibrahim. Fi'l-'alamin, innaka hamidun majid."

(O Allah! Bless Muhammad and the family of Muhammad, as You blessed Ibrahim and the family of Ibrahim and bestow blessings on Muhammad and the family of Muhammad as You bestowed blessings on Ibrahim and the family of Ibrahim. In all the worlds, You are praiseworthy, glorious.)

11) **The First Sitting.** The eleventh is the first sitting after the second *rak'at*.

12) **Resting.** The twelfth is to rest in each position until stillness is obtained.

13) **The Final Sitting.** The thirteenth is to sit in the final *rak'at* of the prayer for the *tashahhud* until the *salam* has been said.

14) **The *Salam* Aloud.** The fourteenth is to say the *salam* aloud.

15) **Returning the *Salam*.** The fifteenth is to return the *salam* of the Imam.

16) **The *Salam* to the Left.** The sixteenth is to repeat the *salam* to the left if there is anyone on the left.

17) **Following the Calls.** The seventeenth is to follow the calls of the one who calls out behind the Imam.

18) ***Sutra*.** The eighteenth is the *sutra* (barrier). It should be at least the thickness of a lance and the length of a forearm, free of any impurity and firmly planted in the ground.

The Description of the Prayer

You start by making the intention for the particular prayer you are about to perform and then, raising your hands to about the height of your shoulders, you say, "*Allahu Akbar*" and lower your hands to your sides. Then you recite the *Fatiha* followed by a *sura* or other piece of Qur'an. During the recitation you stand upright with your head level and your eyes lowered. When you have finished reciting the *sura* you say, "*Allahu Akbar*" and go into *ruku'* (bowing position). In *ruku'* you place your hands on your knees and your back should be more or less parallel with the ground. You do not raise or lower your head and your arms should be slightly away from your sides. While in *ruku'* you glorify Allah saying, "*Subhana rabbiyi'l-'adhim*," (Glory be be to my Lord the Great) three times. Then you stand upright again, saying, "*Sami'a'llahu liman hamidah. Rabbana wa lakal-hamd.*" (Allah hears the one who praises Him. Our Lord to you belongs all praise.) If the prayer is being led by an Imam, he says the first half and those following him respond with the second half.

Then, saying "*Allahu Akbar*", you go down into *sujud* (prostration), placing your hands on the ground before your knees. Your forehead and nose should touch the ground. Your hands should be level with your head with the fingers slightly apart pointing toward *qibla* and your arms should be away from your body with the elbows well off the ground, like outspread wings. Your feet should be upright with the toes bent forward. While in *sujud* you glorify Allah saying, "*Subhana rabbiyi'l-a'la*," (Glory be to my Lord, the Exalted) three times.

Then you lift yourself up saying, *"Allahu Akbar"*, and sit back. You fold your left foot under you while you sit between prostrations, and you keep your right foot upright. You push yourself up from the *sujud* with your fingertips and lift your hands from the ground onto your knees. Then you prostrate a second time as you did the first time. You then stand by pushing yourself up with your hands. You do not go into a sitting position and then stand up from there. Doing as we have stated, you say *"Allahu Akbar"* as you stand up.

You then recite in the same way as you did before, starting with the *Fatiha* and following it with a *sura* or other passage from the Qur'an which should preferably be slightly shorter than the one you recited in the first *rak'at* and come from later in the Book. You then complete the *rak'at* as you did the first, going into *ruku'*, standing up from it, and going into *sujud* twice as has already been described above. However, this time, after the second *sajda*, you do not stand up but sit back on your left buttock with your left foot under your right leg. While sitting like this you say the *tashahhud*. Your left hand should be placed palm down on your left thigh with the fingers together. Your right hand should be made into a fist and then placed on your right thigh, thumb on top, with your index finger extended and pointing forwards. As you recite the *tashahhud* you move the top half of your index finger back and forth. The text of the *tashahhud* has already been given above.

If the prayer you are doing consists of only two *rak'ats* you now say the *salam* and the prayer is finished. If the prayer is longer you stand upright again after finishing the *tashahhud* and when you have reached the upright position say *"Allahu akbar"*.

You then complete the prayer in the way that has already been described except that you only recite the *Fatiha*. After the *tashahhud* in the final *rak'at* you recite the prayer on the Prophet called the *Salat al-Ibrahimiyya* whose text has also been given above. Then you say the *salam* to end the prayer.

Women do the prayer in exactly the same way as men except that they gather themselves in, keeping their bottoms down and their arms close to their sides.

Things that Invalidate the Prayer

The prayer is invalidated by laughing deliberately or by accident, by doing the prostration of forgetfulness unnecessarily, by adding a *rak'at* or prostration deliberately, by eating or drinking deliberately, or by speaking, unless it is to put the prayer right. It is invalidated by saying a lot instead of a little in this case, by blowing the nose, by ritual impurity, or remembering a missed prayer, by intentional vomiting, by more than four *rak'ats* in the four *rak'at* prayers, and by a prostration which accidently precedes the Imam, and by leaving out the prostration of forgetfulness if three or more *sunnas* have been missed.

Making up Missed Prayers

You must make up any obligatory prayers you have missed in their correct order as soon as you can. The correct order of two outstanding prayers which are due at the same time must be observed. If you diverge from it, you must always repeat the second one. For instance, if you pray *Maghrib* with the Imam without having prayed *'Asr,* you pray *'Asr* after finishing the prayer with the Imam and then pray *Maghrib* again. Missed prayers must precede current ones, even if the time for the current prayer passes, as long as the outstanding prayers are not more than five prayers. If they are more than five, according to one well-known statement, or more than four in another, the current prayer comes first if the time left to do it is short.

If you remember a missed prayer having begun another one, you stop as long as you have not gone into *ruku'.* If you have gone into *ruku',* you add another *rak'at* to it, and finish after an even number. If you are following an Imam, you continue with the Imam and then when the prayer has finished, you pray what you have forgotten and repeat the prayer which you prayed with the Imam. If the prayer which you prayed with the Imam was *Jumu'a* (the Friday Prayer), then you pray *Dhuhr* when you repeat it.

Making up prayers is permitted at any time. Anyone who needs to make up prayers should not do superogatory prayers but spend the time making up the prayers he has missed. This includes the *Duha* (forenoon) prayer and the night prayers of Ramadan. He can only do the *Shafi'* and *Witr* prayers, *Fajr* (before *Subh*), the two *'Ids,* the eclipse-prayer, and the prayer for rain. Anyone who has prayers to make up can make up the prayers together with other people provided that the members of the group are all making up the same prayers. Any difference in days is not taken into account. Anyone who forgets how many prayers he has to make up, prays a number which does not leave him with any doubt.

The Prostration of Forgetfulness

The prostration of forgetfulness is one of the confirmed *sunnas* of the prayer. It consists of two prostrations before the *salam* if you have left out a confirmed *sunna*. You complete them by saying the *tashahhud*, and saying the *salam*. If you have added something to the prayer, you prostrate after your *salam*. If you have left something out and added something as well, you prostrate before the *salam* because decrease dominates increase.

There are three kinds of forgetfulness in the prayer:

1) Sometimes you are forgetful and miss out one of the obligations of the prayer, the prostration of forgetfulness is necessary and you must do it. If you do not remember it until after the *salam* and a long time passes, your prayer is invalidated and you must do it again.

2) Sometimes you are forgetful and miss out one of the meritorious parts of the prayer like the *Qunut* supplication, or "Our Lord, praise is Yours" and *"Allahu Akbar"* or something like that. If you prostrate for that before the *salam*, then you invalidate your prayer and must do it again.

3) Sometimes you are forgetful and miss out one of the *sunnas* of the prayer like the *sura* with the *Fatiha*, the two *tashahhuds*, the sitting, or something like that. You should prostrate for that before the *salam*.

If you forget to do the prostration before the *salam* and say the *salam,* you can do the prostration provided you do it straight away. If some time elapses before you remember then the prayer is invalidated and you must do the whole prayer again.

The prostration after the *salam* should not be omitted and you should do it even if you only remember it after two months have passed. If you put the prostration after the *salam* before it your prayer is not invalidated.

If you do not know whether you have prayed three or two, you build on what you are certain about and do what you have doubts about, and then prostrate after the *salam.*

The Imam

Among the conditions of the Imam is that he be a Muslim, rational, just, mature, and know what is necessary for the validity of the prayer in recitation and *fiqh.* If you follow an Imam, and then it becomes clear to you that he is a *kafir*, a woman or a hermaphrodite, insane, wantonly engaged in wrong, a child who has not yet reached puberty, or someone in a state of ritual impurity (*hadath*) who knows about the impurity and yet prays in spite of it, or has knowledge of it during the prayer and yet continues, then your prayer is invalidated and you must do it again. The Imam is not permitted to be higher than those following him except by a very small amount - like a handspan or there about. Those following the Imam can be higher than the Imam, even by a floor. If the Imam or the one following him intends to elevate the Imam excessively, then the prayer is invalidated. It is not a condition for the Imam to intend to be Imam except in four cases:

1) The *Jumu'a* prayer.
2) Joining prayers.
3) The prayer of appointing a Khalif.
4) The fear-prayer.

Some of them add all congregational prayers to that, but there is disagreement about it.

Unit 8: Fasting

Fasting (*sawm*) is obligatory on every Muslim over the age of puberty for the entire month of Ramadan. Women who are menstruating or in the period of post-natal bleeding do not fast but must make up the days they miss later. The same applies to those who are ill or on a journey. Women who are pregnant or breast-feeding are also permitted to postpone the fast if they fear for their own health or that of their baby.

The Obligations of Fasting

There are two obligations of fasting:

1) **Intention.** No fasting is valid without it, whether obligatory or superogatory. It is also a condition that it be specific. For example, you must clearly intend to perform the obligation of fasting Ramadan. A conditional intention is invalid. If you were to make an intention on the Night of Doubt to fast the next day if it were to be part of Ramadan, your fast would not be valid because the intention was conditional.

2) **Abstention.** The second is to abstain from anything which breaks the fast, like sexual intercourse, anything which might cause emission of sperm or prostatic fluid, intentional vomiting, injections, or eating and drinking, between the time from the first light of dawn to sunset.

The *Sunnas* of Fasting

The *sunnas* of fasting are three:

1) Hastening to break the fast as soon after sunset as possible.
2) Delaying the pre-dawn meal until shortly before dawn.
3) Keeping the tongue from superfluous speech and all the limbs from wrong action.

Unit 9: Zakat

Zakat is an annual payment taken from livestock, certain kinds of agricultural produce, and monetary wealth and goods provided they exceed a certain minimum amount (*nisab*) and have been owned for at least one year. It is obligatory on all Muslims whatever their age, conditional on absolute ownership of the property concerned. The actual amount is dependant on the particular kind of property. In the case of monetary wealth it is one fortieth. It should be distributed among certain categories of people including the very poor and those in urgent need.

The Obligations of *Zakat*

The obligations of *zakat* are three:
1) **Intention.** The first is a clear intention that what is being paid out is to fulfil the obligation of *zakat*.
2) **Promptness.** The second is not delaying *zakat* beyond the time that it is due.
3) **Non-transferability.** The third is that *zakat* must be paid by the individual who owes it. It is not permissible to transfer the obligation to someone else, for instance a debtor who owes you money.

The *Adab* of *Zakat*

The *adab* of *zakat* are three:

1) **Equanimity.** The first is that you should not show any reluctance in parting with what you owe for *zakat* and be happy to fulfil your obligation.
2) **Quality.** The second is that the produce, livestock or property used to pay *zakat* should be of good quality.
3) **Concealment.** The third is that whenever possible it is good to conceal your payment from the sight of others.

Unit 10: *Hajj*

Hajj is the journey to Makka and the fulfilment of the rites of *Hajj* during the designated days of the month of *Dhu'l-Hijja*. It is obligatory on all Muslims, male and female once in a lifetime if they are able to undertake it. The ability to undertake it is conditional on their having sufficient wealth to cover the cost of the journey and look after those that they are responsible for during their absence, on their state of health being good enough to withstand the rigours of the journey, and on the way there being open and free from excessive danger.

The Obligations of *Hajj*

The obligations of the *Hajj* are four:

1) The first is the *ihram*.
2) The second is the *Tawaf al-Ifada*.
3) The third is going (*sa'y*) between Safa and Marwa.
4) The fourth is standing at 'Arafat.

The *Sunnas* of *Hajj*

The *sunnas* of the *Hajj* are twelve:

Four of them are connected with the state of *ihram*:

1) The first is the *ghusl* preceding it.
2) The second is using unsewn material for the lower wrapper, the upper wrapper, and the sandals.
3) The third is two *rak'ats* when entering into the state of *ihram*.
4) The fourth is reciting the *talbiya*.

Four are connected with *tawaf* (circling the Ka'ba):

1) The first is walking.
2) The second is kissing the Stone with the lips.
3) The third is continuous *du'a* (supplication).
4) The fourth is the half-run for men, but not for women.

Four are connected with *sa'y* (going between Safa and Marwa):
1) The first is kissing the rock.
2) The second is running in the middle of the valley for men.
3) The third is climbing up Safa and Marwa.
4) The fourth is *du'a.*

Section: The Description of *Hajj*

Those intending to go on *hajj* should enter the state of *ihram* after an obligatory or superogatory prayer. They should have a *ghusl*, making a clear intention for whatever type of *hajj* or *'umra* they are intending to perform and then put on the garments of *ihram*. In the case of men these consist of two unsewn sheets one round the waist and one over the shoulders and in the case of women simple full-length dress, preferably white. Women must not cover their faces in *ihram*. In *ihram* it is forbidden to hunt game, to kill lice or similar creatures, to have sexual contact of any kind, to fight or quarrel, to contract or perform a marriage, to shave or remove hair in any way, to cut the nails and to use scent or beautify the body in any way.

After going into *ihram* you should recite the *talbiya* saying, "*Labbayk, Allahumma, labbayk, labbayka la sharika laka labbayk, inna'l-hamda wa'n-ni'mata laka wa'l-mulk. La sharika lak.*" (At your service, Allah, at

Your service! At Your service, You have no partner, at Your service! All praise and blessings belong to You as well as the kingdom. You have no partner.) It is also recommended to have a *ghusl* before entering Makka.

The *talbiya* continues to be said during the journey to Makka after the prayers, at every sunrise, when groups of people are encountered and periodically throughout the journey but it is not necessary to be too insistent about it. When you enter Makka, you stop reciting the *talbiya* until after you have completed *tawaf* and *sa'y*. Then you can resume saying it until the sun passes the meridian on the Day of 'Arafat and you go to the prayer-place there. It is recommended to enter Makka by Kada'th-Thaniya which is above Makka, and to leave Makka by Kuda. If you do not do so, there is no objection. Malik said, "When he enters Makka, let him enter the mosque," so it is good to go to the *haram* as soon as possible after arriving in Makka. If possible enter it by the gate of Banu Shayba.

You first make for the Black Stone and kiss it if you can can. If not, you should touch it with your hand and if even that is not possible you should gesture towards it. Then, starting from the Black Stone corner, you do *tawaf* of the House circling it anti-clockwise seven times - three times at a half-run and four times walking normally, kissing or touching the Black Stone every time you pass it, or gesturing towards it, saying, "*Allahu Akbar*". You should also honour the Yamani corner but only by touching it with your hand. When your *tawaf* is complete, you do two *rak'ats* at the Station of Ibrahim. Then you touch the Stone again if you can and it is also recommended to drink some water from the well of Zamzam.

Then you go to Safa, climb up it and stand on it making *du'a*. From there you walk to Marwa, running in the middle section of the valley between the green markers. When you reach Marwa, you climb up it and stand on it making *du'a*. Then you go back to Safa. You do this seven times ending up at Marwa. If your original intention was for *'umra* alone or *hajj at-tamattu'* your *'umra* is completed and you now shave your head or cut off some of your hair and come out of the state of *ihram*. If your intention was for *hajj al-ifrad* or *hajj al-qiran* you remain in *ihram*.

Then on the Day of *Tarwiya* (watering), the eighth day of *Dhu'l-Hijja*, you go out to Mina where you pray the *Dhuhr, 'Asr, Maghrib, 'Isha'*, and *Subh* prayers. After *Subh* you go on to 'Arafat, continuing to say the *talbiya* all the time until the sun reaches the meridian when you go to the place of prayer, having already done *wudu'*. There you join together *Dhuhr* and *'Asr* behind the Imam, and then you go to the Stopping-place at 'Arafat where you stay until the sun sets.

Then, without praying, you make your way as quickly as possible to Muzdalifa where you join together *Maghrib* and *'Isha'*. You stay the night there and while there pick up forty-nine or seventy small stones (depending on whether you intend to spend two or three days at Mina). After praying *Subh* at Muzdalifa and standing at the *Mash'ar al-Haram*, you set off for Mina, going as quickly as you can. When you reach Mina, you stone the *Jamra al-'Aqaba* with seven of the stones you have collected which should be no larger than the size of peas. You say, "*Allahu Akbar*" with each pebble as you throw it.

If you are going to sacrifice an animal you do it at this point. You then have your head shaved after which you return to Makka to do the *Tawaf al-Ifada*. Once you have completed the *Tawaf al-Ifada* you come out of *ihram* and all the things which were forbidden become permissible again so that you can groom yourself and wear normal clothing. You then return to Mina for either two or three days depending on how much time you have available. When the sun is at the meridian on each of the days, you stone each of the *Jamrat* in turn, throwing seven pebbles at each and saying, *"Allahu Akbar"* with each pebble as you throw it. After stoning the *Jamra al-'Aqaba* you remain standing a while in order to make *du'a*. After you have completed the stoning on your last day in Mina, you return to Makka and your *hajj* is then completed.

Before leaving Makka you do the *Tawaf* of Farewell, as near as possible to your final departure. It is recommended for those leaving Makka after *hajj* or *'umra* to say:

"A'ibuna ta'ibuna 'abiduna hamiduna sajiduna li-Rabbina. Saddaqa'llahu wa'dahu wa nasara 'abdahu wa hazama'l-ahzaba wahdah."

(Returning, turning in repentance, worshipping, praising, prostrating to our Lord. Allah has confirmed His promise, helped His slave, and routed the enemy parties alone.)

O Allah! Give us success in following the *Sunna* of our Prophet Muhammad, may Allah bless him and grant him peace.

The first part is finished. It is the Science of *Fiqh*.

2
IMAN
The Science of *Tawhid*

Each responsible person must learn enough of the doctrines of *tawhid* to make his belief firm.

Unit 1: What is necessary for Allah

Each responsible person must know that Allah necessarily exists, is before-time (*qadim*), going-on (*baqi*), separate from events-in-time (*mukhalaqa'l-hawadith*), entirely self-sustaining (*ghani*), and One in His essence, attributes, and actions (*ahad*). He has power (*qudra*), will (*irada*), knowledge (*'ilm*), life (*hayat*), hearing (*sam'*), sight (*basira*) and speech (*kalam*). He is Powerful (*qadir*), Willing (*murid*), Knowing (*'alim*), Living (*hayy*), Hearing (*sami'*), Seeing (*basir*), and Speaking (*mutakallim*).

Unit 2: What is impossible for Allah

Each responsible person must know that the opposites of these necessary things are impossible for Allah. They are: non-existence, in-timeness, annihilation, connection to events in-time, need of other-than-Himself, incapacity, coercion, ignorance, death, deafness, sightlessness, dumbness or that He should be powerless, reluctant, ignorant, dead, deaf, blind or dumb.

Unit 3: What is conceivable for Allah

Each responsible person must also know that the doing or leaving undone of any possible thing is conceivable for Him. None of them are necessary or impossible for Him.

Unit 4: What is necessary for the Messengers, blessings and peace be upon them

Each responsible person must also know that truthfulness, fulfilling the trust, and conveying what they are commanded to convey to creation are necessary qualities of the Messengers, blessings and peace be upon them.

Unit 5: What is impossible for the Messengers, blessings and peace be upon them

Each responsible person must also know that the opposites of these three attributes are impossible for the Messengers, blessings and peace be upon them. They are: lying, treachery, and concealing what they are commanded to convey. They cannot do these things, either intentionally or inadvertently.

Unit 6: What is conceivable for the Messengers, blessings and peace be upon them

Each responsible person must also know what is

conceivable for the Messengers, blessings and peace be upon them, by way of non-essential human characteristics which do not lead to any imperfection in their exalted ranks - like illness (other than insanity), blindness, leprosy or other imperfections. Eating, drinking, marriage, buying and selling are also conceivable for them, blessings and peace be upon them.

Unit 7: The proof of the necessary attributes of Allah and of what is impossible and conceivable for Him

Our proof of His existence is that He brings creatures out of non-existence since the non-existent does not have any power to act by itself. Our proof of His before-timeness is His power to bring creatures into existence since the in-time is powerless and cannot act. Our proof of His going-on forever is the permanence of His before-timeness since whatever is permanent in before-timeness cannot possibily become non-existent. Our proof of His separation from in-time events is His power to bring them into existence because the One who has no like cannot be brought into existence. Our proof of His self-subsistence - His richness beyond dependence on place or doer - is the fact that He must be described by intrinsic meanings and meaningfulness (*al-ma'nawiya*) because an attribute (*sifa*) cannot be described by them. He has no need of a doer because of the permanence of His before-timeness - since what is before-time has no need of a doer. Our proof of His oneness is His bringing creatures into existence because if there was another with Him, there would inevitably be conflict between them. Our proof of His power is the fact of His bringing creatures into existence because something powerless would not be able to bring anything into existence. Our proof of His will is the variety of the types of creatures because someone with no will cannot vary his action. Our proof of His knowledge is the perfection of things since someone who is ignorant of a thing cannot perfect it. Our proof of His life is the fact that power, will and knowledge are necessary qualities possessed by Him since someone dead could never be described by them. Our proof of His hearing, sight and speech is the necessity of His being described by perfection because if He was not described by them, He would be described by their opposites, and they are imperfections. Imperfections are impossible for Him, may He be exalted!

Our proof of His doing actions and leaving them undone is what the nature of reality demands concerning their necessity or impossibility. This is because even if something possible was necessary or impossible intellectually, the possible still could not be transformed into a necessity or impossibility in respect of Him, may He be exalted! That would be an impossibility.

The proof of what is necessary for Him is a proof of the impossibility of what is impossible for Him. The proof of the conceivability of His doing actions or leaving them undone is a proof of the non-existence of their necessity and the non-existence of their impossibility.

Unit 8: The proof of what is necessary for the Messengers, blessings and peace be upon them, and what is impossible and conceivable for them.

Our proof of the truthfulness of the Messengers, blessings and peace be upon them, is Allah's confirming them by miracles, since Allah would not confirm a liar. Our proof of their being trustworthy, blessings and peace be upon them, is the command of Allah to us to imitate what they say and do, because Allah would not order us to follow treachery. Our proof of their conveying, blessings and peace be upon them, what Allah commanded them to convey to creation is the fact that they are trustworthy, since they are protected from all that is prohibited. They do not do anything prohibited at all, either intentionally or by accident.

Our proof of the conceivability of non-essential human characteristics for them, blessings and peace be upon them, is seeing these characteristics happen to them since those who were contemporary with them saw them with these characteristics and transmitted that to those who were not contemporary with them through many independent transmissions.

Our proof of what is necessary for them, blessings and peace be upon them, is the proof of the impossibility of what is impossible for them and the proof of the conceivability of non-essential human characteristics for them, blessings and peace be upon them.

When you have understood all this, you will know that all that was brought by the Messengers is true, and that what they reported is correct, and that Muhammad, may Allah bless him and grant him peace, is Allah's slave and Messenger. All that he brought is true and what he reported is correct - the Books revealed from heaven, the existence of angels, the Last Day, death at a set time, the questioning of Munkar and Nakir in the grave, punishment or bliss in the grave, the raising of the dead, their gathering in one place on the Day of Rising, the Reckoning, the Bringing of the Books, the weighing of actions, the intercession, the *Sirat, Kawthar,* the Garden and the Fire, that the believers will see Him and other things which are mentioned in detail in the Book and *Sunna.*

O Allah! Give us success in following the *Sunna* of our Prophet Muhammad, may Allah bless him and grant him peace.

The second part of this book is finished, and it is the Science of *Tawhid.*

3
IHSAN
the Science of *Tasawwuf* (Sufism)

Each responsible person must learn enough of this science to enable him to acquire praiseworthy qualities and to keep him from blameworthy qualities.

Unit 1: The purification of the heart from the whisperings of Shaytan

This is achieved by four things:

1. Seeking refuge with Allah from Shaytan and rejecting those thoughts which originate from him.
2. Remembering Allah with the heart and the tongue.
3. Reflecting on the proofs of the people of the *Sunna*. These are not those of the philosophers or the *Mu'tazilites*.
3. Questioning those who have true knowledge of the *Sunna*.

Unit 2: The purification of the heart from conceit (*'ujb*)

Conceit is one of the blameworthy qualities which it is forbidden to have. Allah says, *"Do not praise yourselves. He has more knowledge of the one who has fearful awareness."*

Much harm arises out of conceit. Conceit leads to pride, forgetting wrong actions, presumption about acts of *'ibada*, forgetting the blessing of Allah, self-deception, feeling safe from the anger of Allah, believing that you have a station with Allah, and self-justification through action, thought and knowledge. These and things like them are part of the harm which results from conceit.

As far as its reality is concerned, you should know that, without a doubt, conceit comes from an attribute of perfection. A man may have one of two states in his self-perfection of knowledge and *'ibada*.

One state is that he is fearful that what he has obtained will vanish, be uprooted, and stripped away from him. Such a person is not conceited. The other state is that he is not fearful about it vanishing. He is happy about it because it is a blessing from Allah, not because it is related to himself. He also is not conceited.

There is, however, a third state which constitutes conceit. This is when has no fear concerning what he has. He is happy with it and sure of it. His joy in it is because it is a perfection and a blessing, not because it is a gift from Allah. His joy in it is because it is his attribute and it is attributed to him. His joy is not because it is related to Allah since it comes from Him. Conceit is presumption about blessing, relying on it, and forgetting its relationship to the Giver of blessing. This clarifies the reality of conceit.

As far as its cure is concerned, know that the cure for every fault lies in its opposite. The fault in conceit lies in pure ignorance. Its cure is recognition and knowledge which is in direct opposition to that ignorance. A man's conceit is of two kinds: one is regarding those things in which he can exercise his own choice - like the prayer, fasting, *zakat, hajj, sadaqa,* and improving his character. Conceit of this kind is more prevalent. The other is regarding things in which he has no choice - like beauty, power and lineage.

Sometimes someone has both kinds of conceit because he possesses these things and is the locus of their manifestation. This is pure ignorance because the locus is inert and cannot be party to its own bringing-into-existence. How then can someone be conceited about something which is not really his?

On the other hand, he may be conceited because the acts of worship have been performed by his own power which is in-time. This is also pure ignorance as he will see if he considers his power and all the means by which he has it. He acts as if it belonged to him. However, it is all Allah's blessing to him and he has no inherent right to it. He should in fact rejoice in the generosity of Allah since it is He who showered him with what he did not deserve and bestowed it on him, preferring him above others without any antecedent cause or any particular merit on his part.

The truth is that you, your movements, and all of your attributes are part of Allah's creation and invention. You did not act when you acted, and you did not pray when you prayed, for the reality is that, as Allah says in the Qur'an, *"you did not throw when you threw. Allah threw."* Therefore, the worshipper's conceit about his acts of worship is meaningless. It is the same with the conceit of the beautiful person about his beauty, and the conceit of the wealthy man about his riches and generosity.

You suppose that the action is achieved by your own power, but where does your power comes from?

Action is only possible by virtue of your existence and by the existence of your knowledge, will, power, and the rest of your attributes. All this is from Allah not from you because He is the One who creates power and then gives power to the will, sets causes in motion, distributes obstacles, and facilitates action. One of the marvels is that you can be conceited about yourself, and yet wonder at the generosity of Allah. You should be constantly concerned about yourself and your opinions because He is not impressed by any opinion unless there is evidence for it, and it is conclusively contained in the Book of Allah or in the *Sunna* of Allah's Messenger, or by an intellectual proof.

This clarifies the cure of conceit.

Unit 3: The purification of the heart from pride (*kibr*)

Pride is one of the blameworthy qualities and it is forbidden to have it. Allah said, *"I will turn away from My signs those who are arrogant in the earth without right."*

As far as its reality is concerned, you should know that pride is divided into inward and outward pride. Inward pride is a quality within the self, and outward pride is action which appears through the limbs. The name pride (*kibr*) is more appropriate for the inward quality. As for action, it is the result of that quality, and you should know that the quality of pride usually appears as action. When it appears on the limbs, it is called arrogance (*takabbur*), and when it does not manifest itself, it is called pride (*kibr*). Its basis is that quality in the self which manifests itself in satisfaction and pleasure at seeing the self above

59

anyone towards whom a person considers himself superior.

Mere self-exaltation does not make someone arrogant. He might well exalt himself while seeing that another person is greater than him or his equal. In this case, he is not overbearing toward him. Nor is it enough merely to disdain others. In spite of his disdain, a person might still see himself as more despicable and therefore he would not be considered arrogant. He must see that he has a rank and someone else has a rank, and then see his rank as above the other's rank. When he exalts his own value in relationship to someone else, he despises the one below him and puts himself above the other's company and confidence.

If it is very extreme, he may spurn the other's service and not even consider him worthy to stand in his presence. If it is less extreme, he may reject his basic equality, and put himself above this other in assemblies, wait for him to begin the greeting, think that it is unlikely that he will be able to fulfil his demands. If he objects, the proud man scorns to answer him. If he warns him, he refuses to accept it. If he answers him back, he is angry. When the proud man teaches, he is not courteous to his students. He looks down upon them and rebuffs them. He is very condescending toward them and exploits them. He looks at the common people as if he were looking at asses. He thinks that they are ignorant and despicable.

There are many actions which come from the quality of pride. They are too many to be numbered. This is the reality of pride.

The harm it does is immense. The *'ulama'* can help but little against it, let alone the common people.

How could its harm be other than great when it comes between a man and all the qualities of the believer? Those qualities are the doors of the Garden. Pride locks all those doors because it is impossible for him to want for the believers what he wants for himself while there is anything of self-importance in him.

It is impossible for him to have humility - and humility is the beginning of the qualities of those who guard themselves out of fear of Allah - while there is any self-importance in him. It is impossible for him to remain truthful while there is self-importance in him. It is impossible for him to abandon envy while there is self-importance in him. It is impossible for him to abandon anger while there is self-importance in him. It is impossible for him to contain rancour while there is self-importance in him. It is impossible for him to offer friendly advice while there is self-importance in him. It is impossible for him to accept friendly advice while there is self-importance in him. He is not safe from contempt and slander of others while there is self-importance in him. There is no praiseworthy quality but that he is incapable of it from the fear that his self-importance will slip away from him.

As far as its cure is concerned, there are two parts: the knowledge-cure and the action-cure. The remedy can only be effected by joining the two of them. The knowledge-cure is to know and recognise yourself and to know and recognise your Lord. That will be enough to remove your pride. Whoever knows and recognises his own self as it should be known and recognised, knows that it is not worthy of greatness, and that true greatness and pride are only for Allah.

As for gnosis of his Lord and His glory, it is too lengthy a subject for us to discuss here, and it is the goal of the knowledge of unveiling.

Self-recognition is also a lengthy subject. However, we will mention what will help you towards humility and submissiveness. It is enough for you to grasp one *ayat* of the Book of Allah. The knowledge of the first and the last is in the Qur'an for whoever has his inner eye opened. Allah says, *"Perish man! How thankless he is! Of what did He create him? Of a sperm-drop. He created him and determined him and then made the way easy for him. Then He makes him die, buries him, and then, when He wills, raises him."*

This *ayat* points to the beginning of man's creation, his end and his middle. Let a man look at that if he desires to understand its meaning.

As for the beginning of man, he was *"a thing unremembered."* He was concealed in non-existence. Non-existence has no beginning. What is lower and meaner than obliteration and non-existence? He was in non-existence. Then Allah created him from the basest of things, and then from the most unclean thing. He created him from earth and then from a sperm-drop, then a blood-clot, then a lump of flesh. Then He made the flesh bones, and then clothed the bones in flesh. This was the beginning of his existence and then he became a thing unremembered. He was a thing unremembered by reason of having the lowest of qualities and attributes since at his beginning, he was not created perfect. He was created inanimate, dead. He neither heard, saw, felt, moved, spoke, touched, perceived or knew. He began with death before his life, by weakness before strength, by ignorance before knowledge, by blindness before sight, by deafness before hearing, by dumbness before speech, by misguidance before guidance, by poverty before wealth, and by incapacity before capacity.

This is the meaning of His words, *"From what did He create Him? Of a sperm-drop. He created him and determined him,"* and the meaning of His words, *"Has there come upon m.... a period when he was a thing unremembered? We created him of a sperm-drop, a mingling, trying him. We made him hearing, seeing. We guided him upon the way, whether he is thankful or unthankful."*

He created him like that at the beginning. Then He was gracious to him and said, *"We made the way easy for him."* This indicates what He wills for him during the period from life to death. Similarly, He said, *"of a sperm-drop, a mingling, trying him. We made him hearing, seeing. We guided him on the way."* The meaning here is that He gave him life after he was inanimate and dead - first from the earth, and then from a sperm-drop. He gave him hearing after he was deaf and gave him sight after he lacked sight. He gave him strength after weakness and knowledge after ignorance. He created his limbs for him with all the marvels and signs they contain after he lacked them. He enriched him after poverty, made him full after hunger, clothed him after nakedness, and guided him after misguidance. Look how He directed him and formed him. Look at how he made the way easy for him. Look at man's overstepping and how thankless he is. Look at man's ignorance and how he shows it.

Allah says, *"Part of His sign is that He created you from earth."* He created man from humble earth and unclean sperm after pure non-existence so that he would recognise the baseness of his essence and thereby recognise himself. He perfected the sperm-drop for him so that he would recognise his Lord by it and know His immensity and majesty by it, and that He is the only one worthy of true greatness and pride. For that reason, He described him and said, *"Have We not given him two eyes and a tongue and two lips, and guided him on the two roads?"*

He first acquainted him with his baseness and said, *"Was he not a sperm-drop extracted?"* Then he was a blood-clot. Then He mentioned His favour and said, *"He created and fashioned and made a pair from it, male and female,"* in order to perpetuate his existence by reproduction, his existence having been first acquired through independent formation.

When you begin in this manner and your states are like this, how can you possibly show arrogance, pride, glory and conceit? Properly speaking, man is the lowest of the low and the weakest of the weak. Indeed, even if Allah had perfected him, delegated His command to him and made his existence go on by his own choice, he would still dare to be insolent and would forget his beginning and his end.

However, during your existence, He has given illnesses power over you, whether you like it or not, and whether you are content or enraged. You become hungry and thirsty without being able to do anything about it. You do not possess any power to bring about either harm or benefit. You want to know something but you remain ignorant of it. You want to remember something and yet you cannot. You do not want to forget something and yet you forget it. You want to direct your heart to what concerns it and yet you are caught up in myriad whisperings and thought. You own neither your heart nor your self. You desire something when it may mean your destruction, and you detest something when it may save your life. You find some foods delicious when they destroy and kill you, and you find remedies repugnant when they help you and save you. You are not secure for a moment, day or night. Your sight, knowledge, and power may be stripped away, your limbs may become paralysed, your intellect may be stolen away, your spirit may be snatched away, and all that you love in this world may be taken from you. You are hard-pressed, abased. If you are snatched away, you are annihilated. A mere slave. A chattel. You have no power over yourself or anyone else. What could be more puny?

If you were to truly recognise yourself, how could you think yourself worthy of pride? If it were not for your ignorance - and this is your immediate state - you would reflect on it. Your end is death as is indicated by His word, *"Then He makes him die and buries him. Then, when He wills, He raises him."* The meaning here is that your spirit, hearing, sight, knowledge, power, senses, perception, and movement are all stripped away. You revert to being inanimate as you were in the first place. Only the shape of your limbs remains. Your body possesses neither faculties nor movement. Then you are placed in the earth and your limbs decay. You become absent after you existed. You become as if you were not, as you were at first for a long period of time.

Then a man wishes that he could remain like that. How excellent it would be if he were left as dust! However, after a long time, Allah brings him back to life to subject him to a severe trial. He comes out of his grave when his separated parts have been joined together, and he steps out to the terrors of the Day of Rising. He is told, "Come quickly to the Reckoning and prepare for the Outcome!" His heart stops in fear and panic when he is faced with the terror of these words even before his pages are spread out and he sees his shameful actions in them. This is the end of the affair. It is the meaning of His word, *"Then when He wishes, He raises him."*

How can anyone whose state this is be arrogant? A moment of freedom from grief is better than arrogance. He has been shown the beginning and the middle of his condition. If his end had appeared to him - and we seek refuge from Allah - perhaps he would have chosen to be a dog or a pig in order to become dust with the animals rather than a hearing, speaking man, and meet with punishment (if he deserves the Fire). When he is in the presence of Allah, then even the pig is nobler than him since it reverts to dust and it is spared the Reckoning and the punishment. Someone with this state at the Rising can only hope for pardon, and he cannot be at all certain about it. How then can he be arrogant? How can he see himself as anything to which excellence is attached? This is the knowledge-cure.

As far as the action-cure is concerned, it is to humble yourself to people in a constrained unnatural manner until it becomes natural for you.

Unit 4: The purification of the heart from false hope (*amal*)

False hope is one of the blameworthy qualities which it is forbidden to have. Allah says, *"Leave them eating and enjoying themselves. False hope diverts them from the outrage which they do."*

Its reality is that your life-energy is directed to the present moment, and you let things slide.

Its cure is to know that throughout your life, false hope will prevent you from hastening to repentance You say, "I will soon turn in repentance. There are still many days ahead." It also prevents you from hastening to obedience. You say, "I will act later. I still have many days left." That continues to harden your heart because you do not remember death and the grave.

Unit 5: The purification of the heart from unjustified anger (*ghadab*)

Anger is one of the blameworthy qualities which it is forbidden to have. Allah says, *"When He put rage into the hearts of those who reject."* The rage of the *Jahiliyya* (the Time before Islam) was anger without any justification. Allah changed the believers by bestowing the *sakina* (tranquillity of heart) on them.

The reality of anger is the boiling of the blood of the heart in search of revenge. If a man is angry at someone below him, the blood expands and rises to his face and makes it red. If he is angry with someone above him, the blood contracts from his outer skin to his heart and it becomes sorrow. For that reason, he becomes pale. If he is uncertain, the blood is between contraction and expansion.

There are three degrees of anger:

1) Insufficient (*tafrit*).
2) Excessive (*ifrat*).
3) Moderate (*i'tidal*)

Insufficient anger is blameworthy because you are not angry enough to protest against the *haram* - in respect of your wife, for example, or mother if you have no jealousy. Jealousy was created as a protection for man. Part of this failing is to be silent when you see objectionable actions. Part of it is also to be incapable of self-discipline, since self-discipline is made effective by bringing anger to bear on your own appetites, so that you are angry at your self when it inclines to base appetites. Lack of anger is therefore blameworthy.

Excessive anger is also blameworthy. It is to be overcome by anger so that there is no coolness left for the management of the intellect and the *deen*, and you no longer have insight, consideration, reflection or choice. Whenever the fire of anger is intense, it will blind the one who is angry, and it will make him deaf to every warning. It may increase until anger penetrates to the very roots of the senses to the extent that you cannot even see. The entire world may become dark for you. Indeed, the fire of anger may become so intense that it burns up the moisture which gives life to the heart. The angry person then dies of rage.

Among the outward effects of excessive anger are: change of colour, intense shaking in the extremities, confused speech, foam appearing at the corners of the mouth, redness, and an ugly mien. This is the effect of anger on the body.

As far as its effects on the tongue are concerned, it is that you speak with insulting language, obscenity, and ugly words which rational people are ashamed to use. Someone who utters them in anger is ashamed of them after his anger has abated. These are the effects of excessive anger on the tongue.

Its effect on the limbs is that you strike, tear, kill and wound if you are in a position to do so, without any consideration. If the object of your anger flies from you, your own anger turns against you yourself, so you tear your own garments and slap your own face. You may hit your hand on the ground and even go beyond the behaviour of someone overwhelmed by drink. You may fall down and not be able to run or stand up through the intensity of your anger. It may come upon you like a fainting spell. You may hit animals and smash a bowl to the ground and act like a madman. You verbally abuse the beast and speak to it, saying, "How long can I endure this from you?" as if you were addressing a rational being. These are the effects of excessive anger on the limbs.

Its effect on the heart is resentment, envy, concealing evil, resolving to divulge secrets, and other ugly things. This is the effect of excessive anger on the heart.

Praiseworthy anger is in moderation. It is the anger which waits for the indication of the intellect and the *deen*. It arises when it is deemed praiseworthy by the *Shari'a*, and it stops when it is criticised by the *Shari'a*. It is the middle way which the Messenger of Allah, may Allah bless him and grant him peace, described when he said, "The best of affairs is their middle."

Whoever has insufficient anger must treat himself until his anger becomes stronger. Whoever lets his anger go to excess must treat himself until both of them return to the middle way between two extremes. That is the Straight Path.

The cure of anger consists in six things:

1) The first is to reflect on the virtues of restraining rancour, and to desire the reward for doing that.

2) The second is to frighten yourself with the punishment of Allah, saying, "The power of Allah over me is greater than my power over this man. If I carry out my anger against him, then what security will I have against the anger of Allah on the Day of Rising?"

3) The third is to reflect and make yourself fear the results of anger in this world if you have no fear of the Next World.

4) The fourth is to reflect on the ugliness of your form when you are angry. Then you will remember someone else's form when he is angry. Reflect as well on how much you resemble a mad dog when you abandon self-restraint, and how much you resemble the *awliya'* when you abandon your anger.

5) The fifth is to reflect on the cause which summons you to revenge. It must be the words of *Shaytan* to you, "This is incapacity and humiliation for you in the eyes of the people."

6) The sixth is to know that your anger arises from your amazement at something which is acting in conformity with the will of Allah. It is almost as if Allah's anger with you is greater than your own anger.

This is the knowledge-cure.

As far as the action-cure is concerned, it is to say when you are angry, "I seek refuge with Allah from the accursed Shaytan." If you are standing, then sit down. If you are sitting, then lie down, and do *wudu'* or *ghusl*.

Unit 6: The purification of the heart from envy (*hasad*)

Envy is one of the blameworthy qualities which it is forbidden to have. Allah says, *"Do they then envy people for what Allah has given them?"*

As for its reality, you should know that envy is only on account of blessings. When Allah bestows a blessing on your brother, it can lead to one of two states in you. One is that you hate that blessing and want it to leave him. This state is called envy. The definition of envy is hatred of blessings being received and wanting them to depart from those who have received them. The second state is that you do not want it to leave him and do not dislike the fact that it exists and remains with someone, but you desire the same for yourself. This is called thinking someone enviable. Envy is anger at the fact that Allah prefers some of His slaves over others.

There are four levels of envy:

1. To want a blessing to leave someone. If that happens, you do not want it to return to him. This is the very limit of malice.
2. To want the blessing to leave someone in the same way that you might desire a fine house, a beautiful woman, or a lofty, wide *zawiyya* which someone else has obtained and which you want for yourself. Your aim is not to remove that blessing. You hate the absence of the blessing, not that it has been bestowed on someone else.
3. Not to desire the blessing itself, but to desire one like it for yourself. If you cannot have one like it, you want it to leave the person who

has it so that the contrast between you will
not be apparent.
4. To desire the same blessing for yourself but if
you do not obtain it, you do not desire it to
leave the person who has it. The last level is
excused if it is something of this world, and it
is recommended if it a matter of the *deen*.

As far as the remedy for envy is concerned, you
should know that envy is one of the serious sicknesses of the heart. Sicknesses of the heart can only be
treated by knowledge and action. Useful knowledge
concerning the sickness of envy is to really recognise
that envy is harmful to you, both in your *deen* and in
this world. There is no harm for one who is envied,
either in this world or in his *deen*. Rather, he profits
by it both in this world and in his *deen*. When you
recognise this with your inner eye - that you are only
an enemy to yourself and a friend to your enemy -
then you will inevitably part company with envy.

As for its being harmful to you in the *deen*, this is
because having envy means that you are angry about
the decree of Allah and you hate the way He has
apportioned blessing to His slaves, and His justice
which He established in His kingdom and which is
hidden in His wisdom and reject it. This is an offence
striking at the core of *tawhid* and is an obstruction in
the path of belief. That in itself would be enough of a
crime against the *deen*. However you also act dishonestly toward one of the believers. You abandon good
counsel and you part company with the *awliya'* of
Allah and the Prophets since they desire good for the
slaves of Allah. You form a partnership with Iblis
and all the unbelievers since they desire that the
believers should experience afflictions and they

desire their blessings to leave them. These are malicious things in the heart. They eat up the good actions of the heart like fire consumes firewood, and obliterate them as the night obliterates the day.

As for its being harmful to you in this world, this is because you are pained and punished by your envy. You are always full of grief and sorrow since Allah does not cease to pour out blessings on your adversaries. Therefore you are constantly being punished by every blessing you see, and you are pained by every affliction which is turned away from them. You are constantly full of sorrow. Your breast is constricted in the manner you desire for your enemies and which your enemies desire for you. You wanted severe trial for your enemies, but now you immediately come to severe trial and sorrow yourself.

Blessing does not leave the envied person because of your envy. Even if you did not believe in the Rising and the Reckoning, it would still show a lack of astuteness on your part. If you are at all intelligent, you should be on your guard against envy because of the pain and evil it contains and its lack of benefit. How much more should this be the case when you know that envy is the cause of intense punishment in the Next World. How astonishing is a man of intellect who exposes himself to the wrath of Allah without obtaining any profit at all from doing so. Indeed, it carries harm and pain which he must endure. His world is destroyed without any gain or benefit for himself.

As for its not having any harmful effect on the envied one either in his *deen* or this world, it is obvious that blessing will not leave him because of someone else's envy. Allah decreed it as good fortune and blessing, so it will certainly last until the time which

Allah decreed for it. There is no way to repel it. Everything is decreed with Him and every term is predetermined.

The one who is envied profits by it both in his *deen* and in this world. It is clear that his profit in the *deen* is that he is wronged by you, especially if you publicise your envy through speech and action, by slandering him and by destroying his reputation and mentioning his bad qualities. It is a gift which you present to him, i.e. by that, you give him your good deeds and so you will meet him bankrupt on the Day of Rising. You will be deprived of blessing then as you were deprived of blessing in this world. It is as if you wished to remove blessing from him while the blessings which Allah bestows on you continue as He gives you success in good deeds. You give these to him and increase him with blessing upon blessing while you multiply misery for yourself.

As for his profit in this world, one of the most important desires of created beings is grief and sorrow for their enemies. No punishment can be greater than that which you experience from the pain of envy. The goal of your enemies is to have blessing while you are sunk in sorrow and loss. You have done to yourself what they desire to do to you. Because of that, your enemy does not desire your death. He desires to prolong your life in the punishment of envy. This is the knowledge-cure.

As far as the action-cure is concerned, you must make yourself do the opposite of what envy calls you to. If it makes you arrogant, you must humble yourself. If it provokes you to withhold, you must yourself give more. This is the action-cure.

As for what is necessary in order to prevent envy in the heart when someone irritates you, you should know that if you want blessing to leave him and you direct your tongue against him, then you are an envier. By your envy, you commit an act of rebellion. If you want the blessing to leave him while you restrain yourself outwardly in every way, but you do not dislike your state, then you are envious and you commit an act of rebellion. This is because envy is an attribute of the heart, not an attribute of action. If you dislike this state by insight, and your restrain your outward actions as well, you have then done what is necessary.

Unit 7: The purification of the heart from showing-off (*riya'*)

Showing-off is one of the blameworthy qualities which it is forbidden to have. Allah says, *"Woe to those who pray and are heedless of their prayers, to those who show off and withhold."*

As far as its reality is concerned, you should know that showing-off (*riya'*) is derived from seeing (*ru'ya*). Its root is to seek reputation in people's hearts. You desire to make them see good qualities in you, and by that, to obtain high rank in their hearts. You can seek high rank by all actions. However, the name "showing-off" specifically refers to seeking high rank in people's hearts through acts of *'ibada*.

It has five divisions:

1. Showing-off with the body. That is by outward emaciation so that people will imagine that that you are intense in your striving. By emaciation, you also want to indicate scarcity of provision.

2. Showing-off through dress and appearance. That is by having dishevelled hair, tattered garments, bowing the head while walking, leaving the mark of prostration on the face, rolling up your garment, and not cleaning it.

3. Showing-off with words. That is to do *dhikr* out loud in the presence of other people, and to command the good and forbid the objectionable in full view of people. It is to manifest anger at objectionable things in the presence of other people, and to move the lips with *dhikr* in full view of other people. It is also to raise the voice pretending that it comes from sorrow and fear.

4. Showing-off by action. That is like someone who prays and shows off by standing for a long time, by spending a long time in *ruku'* and *sajda*, by not turning aside, by keeping still and silent, and by keeping the feet and the palms level. It is the same with fighting in the way of Allah, the *hajj* and *sadaqa*.

5. Showing-off by claiming connection to people. For instance, a man will mention the Shaykhs often in order to show that he has met many Shaykhs and profited from them. He says, "All the Shaykhs I have met," and "I met so-and-so," and "I went about in the land and served the Shaykhs." He talks about everything that has happened to him.

This, and all that preceded is blameworthy since by it, you are seeking high rank and reputation in people's hearts.

As for its cure, you should know that showing-off

is man's nature when he is a child. You can only manage to tame it by intense effort.

There are two parts to its cure. The first is to pluck it out by its roots. These are love of being praised, flight from the pain of criticism, and greed for what other people have. The second is to repel it immediately it manifests itself.

The remedy is to know that showing off is harmful and corrupts the heart. It precludes success and precludes high standing with Allah. It incurs punishment and disgrace to the extent that when you are in front of people, there will be shouts of "You shameless liar! You two-faced deceiver! Weren't you ashamed when you sold obedience to Allah for Allah's hatred out of desire for this world and love of high rank among people? You sought their pleasure in exchange for the wrath of Allah, and you sought nearness to them in exchange for distance from Allah."

If you reflect on this shame, you have no alternative but to turn away from showing-off. At the same time you must direct yourself to dispelling your concern for consideration in the hearts of others. Pleasing people is a goal which you will never attain. If you seek to please them in exchange for the wrath of Allah, Allah will be angry with you.

The cure for the greed of what others have is that Allah is the One who subjects the hearts to withholding or giving. If you concentrate on the bliss of the Next World, you will think very little of anything connected to creation. You should direct your heart towards Allah. By acts of unveiling, things will be shown to you which increase your intimacy with Allah and alienate you from creation. This is the knowledge-cure.

As far as the action-cure is concerned, it is to make yourself conceal your acts of *'ibada* until your heart is content with the knowledge of Allah and to repel any of sign of it that appears, repelling it through dislike of it.

Unit 8: Turning away with regret (*tawba*) from all acts of rebellion

Tawba is one of the praiseworthy attributes which you must acquire. Allah says, *"Turn in tawba to Allah altogether, O believers, so you might prosper."*

Its reality is freeing the heart from wrong actions, which you have done, out of the desire to exalt Allah, the Mighty, the Majestic, and fleeing from His wrath. It must not be from any worldly desire nor from fear of people, seeking praise and renown, or from weakness.

There are three things that will help you to achieve it.

1. To remember the result of ugly wrong actions.
2. To remember the intensity of Allah's punishment.
3. To remember the weakness of your body.

If you persevere in remembering these three things, good counsel will move you to *tawba*, Allah willing.

You should know that in general, wrong actions are of three types:

1. The abandonment of your obligations to Allah - prayer, fasting, *zakat*, *kaffara* (reparation) or anything else of that nature.

2. Wrong actions between you and Allah - like drinking wine, playing wood-wind pipes, consuming usury, and things like that. You regret those actions and keep it in your heart never again to repeat them.
3. Wrong actions between you and the slaves of Allah. They are more difficult, and fall into various categories. They may be connected with property, the person, reputation, respect or the *deen*. You should make reparation for any of these things which were mentioned that you can. If you cannot, you must turn to Allah with humility and sincerity so that He may be pleased with you on the Day of Rising.

Unit 9: Doing-without (*zuhd*) in this world

Zuhd is one of the praiseworthy qualities which you must have. Allah says, *"Do not extend your eyes to what We have given pairs of them to enjoy, the flower of this life."*

Know that there are two types of doing-without: one is a doing-without which is from your own will and the other is a doing-without which is not from your own will. The one which is from your own will has three conditions:

1. To abandon seeking what is lost to you of this world.
2. To part from what you have of it.
3. To abandon will and choice.

The doing-without which is not from your own will is coolness in the heart towards this world.

What will help you towards it is to remember the harm of this world. The decisive word is that this world is the enemy of Allah while you are His lover. If you love someone, you hate his enemy. If you say, "What is the judgement concerning doing-without in this world? Is it obligatory or superogatory?" Know that doing without the *haram* is obligatory, and doing without the *halal* is superogatory. If you say, "We must have a certain amount of this world in order to maintain our strength and proper condition, so how can we do without it?" Know that doing-without concerns the superfluous since your proper condition and strength has no need of this superfluity. The goal is strength and vigour. The goal is not only food, drink and pleasure.

Unit 10: Safeguarding yourself out of fear of Allah (*taqwa*)

Taqwa is one of the praiseworthy qualities which you must acquire. Allah says, *"Whoever obeys Allah and His Messenger and fears Allah and guards himself out of fear of Him, those, they are the successful."*

Its reality is freeing the heart from the wrong actions which you have done in the past. It has four stages:

1. Safeguarding yourself from idolworship.
2. Safeguarding yourself from acts of rebellion.
3. Safeguarding yourself from innovation.
4. To avoid superfluous things.

What will help you to gain it is guarding your five limbs which are the source of your actions. They are: the eye, the ear, the tongue, the heart, and the genitals. You should be careful regarding them and guard them from whatever you fear will harm you in your deen - acts of rebellion, the *haram*, superfluity, and even extravagance in the *halal*. When you attain to safeguarding these limbs, the hope is that it will give you all the support you need.

Unit 11: Trust and reliance in Allah (*tawakkul*)

Tawakkul is one of the praiseworthy qualities which you must acquire. Allah says, *"Whoever relies on Allah, He is enough for him."*

Its reality is confidence and calmness in the heart, and the realisation that the sustenance of your physical structure is by Allah alone. It is not by anyone other than Allah, and it is not by any of the debris of this world nor by any other cause.

What will help you towards it is to remember that Allah guarantees your provision, and that His knowledge and power are perfect, and that He is disconnected from creation and far removed from forgetfulness and from incapacity.

Unit 12: Entrusting your affairs to Allah

Entrusting your affairs to Allah is one is the praiseworthy qualities which you must acquire. Allah says, *"I have entrusted my affair to Allah."*

Its reality is your desire for Allah to preserve you from all that has danger in it and against which you have no security.

What will help you in it is to remember the danger of all affairs, and the possibility of your destruction and corruption. In all of that, you must remember your own incapacity to guard yourself against the blows of danger.

Unit 13: Contentment (*rida'*) with the decree of Allah

Contentment with Allah's decree is one of the praiseworthy qualities which you must acquire. Allah says, *"No affliction occurs except by the permission of Allah. Whoever believes in Allah. his heart is guided."*

Its reality is to abandon anger and to remember that what Allah decrees is better and more appropriate. He does not need to justify its rightness or wrongness. This is one of its conditions. If you say, "Evil is not by the decree of Allah, so how can anyone be content with it?" Know that evil is the result of the decree. It is not the decree itself, and you do not have to be content with it. In fact, it is inconceivable for you to be content with the result of the decree except when it conforms to the *Shari'a*. You must be content with the decree itself, but the decree of evil does not come from evil.

What will help you to gain it is that to remember the wrath of Allah when you are angry, and to remember that He rewards whoever is content with His decree.

Unit 14: Fear and hope (*khawf and raja'*)

Fear and hope are among the praiseworthy qualities which you must acquire. Allah says, *"They hope for His mercy and fear His punishment."*

The reality of this fear is a trembling which is generated in the heart by remembering objectionable things which you have done. It comes to you through thoughts and it is not under your control. You can do things to prepare the way for it. These are four:

1. To remember past wrong actions.
2. To remember the severity of Allah's punishment.
3. To remember your own weakness.
4. To remember the power of Allah over you and that He exerts His power over you when He wills and how He wills.

What will help you to it is to remember how Allah seizes and strips away as He did in the case of Iblis and Ba'lam. You should also remember His words, *"Do you suppose that We created you without a purpose?"* and *"Does man suppose that he will be left to his own devices?"* and other verses like these, which are meant to provoke fear.

As for the definition of hope, it is the joy in the heart when it recognises the over-flowing favour of Allah and the vastness of His mercy. It also comes to you through thoughts, and is not under your control. You can do things to prepare the way for it. These are four:

1. To remember Allah's past favour to you given without intermediary or intercessor.
2. To remember the generosity of the reward He has promised you without your having done anything to deserve it.
3. To remember the abundance of His blessings in respect of your *deen* at the present moment

without your deserving it or asking for it.
4. To remember the vastness of His mercy.

What will help you to it is to remember how Allah pardons as He did in the case of the sorcerers of Pharaoh and the People of the Cave, and to remember His mercy in the verses of the Qur'an, which provoke desire. Allah says, *"He is the One who accepts repentance from His slaves and pardons evil deeds,"* and He says, *"Who will forgive wrong actions except Allah?"* and He says, *"Do not despair of the mercy of Allah. Allah forgives wrong actions altogether. He is the Forgiving, the Merciful,"* and the verses like these which provoke desire.

O Allah! O Forgiving! O Merciful! Forgive us all of our wrong actions by the blessing of Sayyiduna Muhammad, may Allah bless him and grant him peace.

Here ends what we intended to write about the sciences of behaviour consisting of *Tawhid, Fiqh,* and *Tasawwuf.* It has been accomplished by the help of Allah, and His help is excellent.

O Allah! Bless Sayyiduna Muhammad, the opener of what was locked, and the seal of what went before, the helper of the Truth by the Truth, and the guide to Your Straight Path, and on his family to the extent of his proper worth and immense value.

The book ends with praise of Allah and His
good help, and with blessings and peace,
on the Master of the Messengers, Muhammad,
and upon his family and all his Companions,
and peace be upon the Messengers.

Song

by Shaykh Malam an-Nasir al-Kibari

written at his *zawiyya* in Kano, Nigeria, 1397 (1977)

Say "Allah" and leave existence and what it contains.
Remember Him often in all states.
Do not turn to those who play and their plunging
if you desire to reach perfection.
And know that you and all the universe are always
an imagination in an imagination of an imagination.
If it had not been for Allah, created beings
and all their affairs would have been obliterated
and all would have vanished.
If you examine it closely, all that is other-than-Allah
is a mere shadow moved by the hand of the
Supreme One.
Phenomenal beings - both subtle and dense - are
only non-existence, both generally and particularly.
Whoever is not existence by himself in himself
is like the afternoon shadow which appears as
shadows projected from a wall.
If it had not been for the rising of the suns of the
essence of His beauty, its existence would be the
very source of the impossible.
The gnostics are annihilated by Him and they see
only manifestation and *tajalli* in phenomenal being.
They go on by the Majestic.
They do not see anything except for the Proud, the
Supreme.
They see other-than-Him is destroyed in reality
by the brilliance of the light of His supreme majesty.
They look only at the light of His perfection
in the present, past and future.

Glossary

adab:	correct behaviour inward and outward.
Amir al-Mu'minin:	the Commander of the Believers, a title of respect given to the Khalif.
amir:	commander, general, political leader of the community.
awliya':	plural of *wali*. See *wali*.
ayat:	lit. a sign; a verse of the Qur'an.
ba'ya:	homage, allegiance given to a leader.
bayt al-mal:	the communal treasury.
deen:	life-transaction; Allah says in the Qur'an, *"Surely the deen with Allah is Islam."* (3:19)
dhikr:	lit. remembrance, mention. In a general sense all *'ibada* (see below) is *dhikr*. In common usage it has come to mean invocation of Allah by repetition of His names or particular formulae.
dhimmi:	a non-Muslim living under the protection of Muslim rule.
du'a':	making supplication to Allah.
faqih:	pl. *fuqaha'* - a man learned in knowledge of *fiqh* (see below) who by virtue of his knowledge can give a legal judgement (*fatwa*) (see below).
fatwa:	an authoritative legal opinion or judgement made by a *faqih* (see above).
fiqh:	science of the application of the *Shari'a* (see below).

ghusl:	full ablution, involving the washing of the whole body.
hafiz:	someone who has memorized the entire Qur'an.
hajj:	the annual pilgrimage to Makka.
halal:	permitted by the *Shari'a*.
haram:	forbidden by the *Shari'a*.
harbi:	unbeliever living in the Abode of War.
hijra:	emigration in the way of Allah. Islam takes its dating from the *hijra* of the Prophet, may Allah bless him and grant him peace, from Makka to Madina.
'ibada:	act of worship.
Iblis:	Shaytan (Satan).
'Id al-Kabir:	festival at the end of the *hajj*.
ihram:	the conditions in respect of clothing and behaviour adopted by someone on *hajj* or *'umra*.
ijtihad:	lit. to struggle - to exercise personal judgement in legal matters when there is no known precedent.
Imam:	man who leads the prayer, an eminent scholar.
janaba:	state of major impurity requiring *ghusl* (see above).
jihad:	struggle, particularly warfare to establish and defend Islam.
Jumu'a:	the day of gathering, Friday, and particularly the midday prayer on that day.
kafir:	unbeliever.
karamat:	lit. tokens of honour, miracles.

Kawthar:	it is said that it is a river in the Garden, abundant blessing, intercession, the Prophet's Basin, etc.
madh-hab:	a school of *fiqh* (see above). There are four main *madh-habs*: Hanifi, Maliki, Shafi'i and Hanbali.
muhtasib:	someone who oversees things.
mujtahid:	someone who is qualified to use *ijtihad*, i.e. make independent decisions in judgements (see above).
Munkar:	an angel who questions those in the grave.
Nakir:	an angel who questions those in the grave.
qadi:	a judge.
qunut:	a supplication done while standing in the prayer.
qibla:	the direction faced in prayer, which is towards the Ka'ba in Makka.
rak'at:	a unit of prayer, a complete series of standing, bowing, prostrations and sittings.
ruh:	the spirit which gives life; the angel Jibril.
ruku':	action of bowing in the prayer
sa':	a measure of volume equal to four double handfuls (*mudds*).
sadaqa:	giving in the way of Allah.
sajda:	position of prostration in the prayer.
salam:	see *taslim*.
sa'y:	a rite of *hajj* and *'umra* involving walking between the two hills of Safa

	and Marwa adjacent to the Sacred Mosque in Makka.
Shari'a:	lit. a road. It is the legal modality of a people based on the revelation of their Prophet. The last *Shari'a* in history is that of Islam. It abrogates all previous *shar'ias*.
Sirat:	the narrow bridge in the Next World which must be crossed to enter the Garden.
sujud:	prostration in the prayer
Sunna:	pl. *sunan* - lit. a form, the customary practice of a person or group of people. It has come to refer almost exclusively to the practice of the Messenger of Allah, Muhammad, may Allah bless him and grant him peace, but also comprises the customs of the First Generation of Muslims in Madina.
sura:	a large unit of Qur'an linked by thematic content, composed of *ayats* (see above). There are 114 *suras* in the Qur'an.
tajalli:	manifestation, "epiphany".
talbiya:	the calling of *'labbayk'* (at your service), on the *hajj*.
takbir:	saying the words, *"Allahu akbar"* (Allah is greater), particularly in the prayer.
tasawwuf:	Sufism.
tashahhud:	lit. to make *shahada* (witnessing). In the context of the prayer it is a formula which includes the *shahada* which is said in the final sitting position of each two *rak'a* (see above) cycle.

taslim:	giving the greeting, *"as-salamu 'alaykum"* (peace be upon you). Prayer ends with a *taslim*.
tawaf:	circling the Ka'ba, done in sets of seven circuits.
tawhid:	the science of the Unity of Allah.
tayammum:	purification done with earth in place of *wudu'*.
'ulama':	scholars.
umm walad:	a slavegirl who has borne her master a child. She cannot be sold and becomes free when her master dies.
'umra:	the lesser pilgrimage. It can be peformed at any time of the year.
wali:	someone who is a "friend" of Allah, someone close to Allah.
wudu':	ritual washing to be pure for the prayer.
zakat:	annual poor tax paid on standing wealth, agricultural produce nd live-stock.
zawiyya:	small religious centre, based around a *wali*, where his followers meet.

CPSIA information can be obtained
at www.ICGtesting.com
Printed in the USA
LVHW101024120423
744156LV00001B/6